THE
PSYCHOLOGY
OF
NETWORK MARKETING

~•~

Twenty Dynamic Principles
of
Leadership and Success

KELTON DREW EARL

Published by
CallOut Publishing, LLC
P.O. Box 107, Draper, Utah 84020

Distributed by
Dream Builders
www.dreambldrs.com

The *Psychology of Network Marketing* is available
on CD and Audio Cassette from Dream Builders.

To order or for additional products
visit our web site or call 1-888-925-5150.

"From my 32-years involvement in all facets of network marketing, the points made in this book emphasize the attributes that are most important to a fulfilling and joyful experience in this industry. I appreciate the opportunity for a good read and reinforcement of the reasons I have remained in this chosen field."
~ Larry Proffit, Senior Vice President
Nikken

"During my 17 years in network marketing, I have never endorsed a book until now. This is a must read for every serious person, in or out of network marketing, who wants to be a leader."
~ Dan McCormick
Network Marketing Professional

"Drew commands your attention. You can feel the power of his words. A believable presenter with a message always tailored to his audience. Dynamic without overpowering, he transfers knowledge based on experience and study with a lighthearted approach. You will not fall asleep when Drew is speaking."
~ Charles W. Parker, Colonel USAF (Ret.)

"If you desire to be a successful leader in Network Marketing (or Direct Sales), reading and following the principles in this book is a must!"
~ Rod C. Yanke, Founder & Chairman
Enviro-Tech International

"Have you ever struggled with the question 'How do I get from where I'm at to where I want to be?' Drawing on a lifetime of personal experiences, Drew Earl has helped thousands find the answer to that question. With empathy and compassion, with insight and inspiration, Drew will connect you with your dreams and change your life forever, he has mine."
~ Dr. Glenn A. Partridge, D.C.

"While it is often said that a picture is worth a thousand words, when Drew Earl speaks he creates thousands of pictures. He is a master painter creating a vivid picture; no, a movie with all its colors, actions and sounds. He helps all that hear or read his words see a world that they can have—if they only believe it as they see it. Drew is a virtuoso of communication and motivation."
~ Jim McNeely, Director
Personal Development Quest

Acknowledgements

In undertaking the task of writing a book, the first feelings of exuberance are quickly extinguished as the labor begins. The easy part is spilling out all the information gained over a twenty-year career onto computer keys. The hard part is the countless hours of support that is provided by the editors, advisors, and supporters of the project. My deep thanks go out to all the people who have inspired me over the years, especially to my mentor, the late Cavett Robert and his dear wife, Trudy; to my wife Gabriela (Gabi), not only for her wonderful contributions, but her encouragement and persistent belief in me; to Tippy Tan, whose brilliant service as an administrative assistant to this project made the impossible, possible; also, to Jerry Thorne, Patrick Hosmer and Steven M. Covey for their dedicated service. I wish to acknowledge Jim Adams, Ira Earl, Jr., Jim McNeely and my late father, Ira L. Earl, Sr., for the wisdom they have shared with me. Lastly to my children, starting with my two youngest Carlo René, and Sasha, for obeying the "Do Not Disturb" sign. To Erika Patriz for her wonderful support and feedback. And to Marlo and Dany for giving me parental challenges sufficient to make any man lock himself in an office and write a book. Finally, thank you to everyone who supports the *Wealth Building Industry*, especially the tens of thousands of distributors I have had the pleasure of knowing and working with over the past ten years.

> *There is a tide in the affairs of men*
> *Which if taken at the flood,*
> *Leads on to fortune;*
> *On such a full sea, we are now afloat.*
> *~ Shakespeare*

My fortune is the companionship of my partner in life,
to whom this work is dedicated, my precious wife,

Gabriela

Thank you for always standing by my side
and saying, "yes," when the tide is at the flood.

Foreword

If I were to find a theme you could hold on to as you begin your journey through these pages, it would be that *"Success needs no explanation and Failure permits no alibi."*

This is a book written for the advanced Network Marketing distributor. It offers no system, and with one exception, it is oriented strictly to the principles of leadership. The exception is the detailed defining of the Network Marketing/MLM Industry versus what I call the *Wealth Building Industry.*

There is no table of contents for two reasons:

One, there is a temptation on the part of the quasi-expert to pick and choose a chapter that he or she may feel is all they need to satisfy curiosity as to whether or not the book follows their particular building philosophy. This book requires reading from beginning to end and for that reason, it is not a particularly long book. The first part is academic in nature and more difficult to read. The remainder of the book is oriented toward the spirit of leadership and the deeper meaning of service. For simplicity of reading, pronouns are in the masculine gender, however both genders are implied.

Two, this book is written from my heart to yours. As you wander through the principles, I want you to feel that you are listening to me, instead of reading me. I would hope that you would mark up the book with notes and under-linings. Every page should be marked up. I would hope that you would use the book in your training. Steal the book's precepts with wild abandon and expound on them as you excel in your careers.

I hope that the book will stir some controversy from time to time, causing you to investigate other writings and teachings about our new industry, and your place in it as a leader.

Most of all, I hope this book heightens your desire to take chances and risk — not necessarily in terms of money, but in terms of personal vulnerability. I hope it chases you out of the security mode, into the adventure mode. Security, when used as a crutch, is like a cancerous sore that ruins our future, dams our river of progress and pays our mortgage to live in the city of compromise. I believe in you and yet, we may never have met. I believe in you, because you paid to obtain this book, or someone believed in you enough to give you a copy. That makes you a winner.

Look around you. The world is full of people that are not just like you. They need a leader. They need you and your leadership. For a short time, let us sit down together and share a journey into the *"WHAT IF"* zone. Perhaps something you may read here will stir the wisdom you have already gained in life and create new horizons of possibilities.

My mentor, Cavett Robert taught me that there is no excuse for effort except for action; there is no reason for action except for results. So it is, you must have a plan of action that accompanies this book, or it will just be mind candy for you, enjoyable for the moment, but lost after tasted.

Cavett also taught me that success in life can only be achieved by organizing my efforts in a definite pattern and directing them toward a specific goal. He quoted Sidney J. Harris on this point:

"A thought that does not fulfill itself in some act, is not a full thought; just as an act that is not preceded by some thought is not a true act, but merely an agitation, an excitement, a spasm of movement. The two are inextricably linked together, making a whole.

A man of action would be a beast, not a man, if he excluded the act of thinking. And a man of thought would be a vegetable, not a man, if he refused to act on his thoughts."

Here is the plan of *action* you can employ. Purchase a package of 3x5 cards and copy the action phrases onto them. These cards are to be carried in your front pocket, or change purse. The point is that the card needs to be read frequently, until it is memorized. And by having it in your change pocket, it will be a nuisance to you. So the sooner you memorize it, the sooner you can throw it away.

This is a first test of true leadership. You are a leader, or a leader in embryo. Any excuse not to do the exercise is a good reason; you're too busy, you've done it before, it's not cool, you don't do 3x5 cards, it's just not you. All of these are excellent reasons. (Your spouse may be making beef curry for dinner, and that is a good reason too!) Any reason will do. But, if you do not do it, you do not get it! You are choosing not to use the action plan of the book. It is just a principle of leadership that you will be missing, a very important principle that says a leader will *do whatever it takes* and not pick and choose actions that are comfortable to do. It is a test of discipline, not a value judgement. Whether or not you decide to do the action plan of the book has nothing to do with you being a fantastic human being. It is an issue dealing with your readiness to *do whatever it takes* to attain leadership skills. As you create these cards, put them in a stack where you can begin the process of diminishing the pile. As you internalize each card and throw it away, you'll be symbolically watching the forces that hold you back slowly melt away.

3 x 5 CARD

> *Leaders are willing to*
> *do whatever it takes*
> *to achieve their worthy goals.*
> *I am such a leader.*
> *(Offer some service today.)*

Psychological Principle #1
LEADERS READ EVERYTHING!

You probably have fifteen or twenty books on how to build a Network Marketing/MLM business. Most likely they are dog-eared and worn out from use. Oh, boy! Now you are going to read *another* one?

One book told you *whom* to sponsor, another told you *how*. The second corrected the first one and explained what was wrong with its philosophy. Then came the rebuttals, writers admitting they were wrong with the first books, but now they have repented and changed their ways. I have just finished reading such a book. Some authors have told you that building a business is like baking a pie, and others have said it is like constructing a building. Some have lauded their earning credits, saying they earned a kabillion pazoozals in their first month, while others say the truth is, it takes years. Let's not leave out the reports of their qualifications. One professes the shortest record, while another claims the longest. One earned it all with two organizations, another with forty. One did it with only first level distributors, another working depth. One did it with products, another with services. They are qualified, because their residual income is one quarter of a million a year, (or was it a month? a day?) Another never earned anything. Interestingly, they all say only positive things about each other to stay in the good graces of the industry promoters.

Nevertheless, it seems they cannot agree on any particular sponsoring and building strategy that will work for everyone. The reason is the things they teach worked for them, and for their particular organization, but may not work for others. It's enough to make you want to deliver pizzas in your spare time.

You hang in there and keep reading, because you know the dream is possible. If only you could sift through the words long enough to find the way that works for you.

The reason I wrote this book is to psychologically help you make it through the sifting process.

This book IS for everyone, and its principles fit all systems for building. It is an educational book for, and about YOU!

The *Psychology of Network Marketing* is directly written for the person who wants the benefits of Network Marketing (such as financial or time freedom), but has two major fears. First is the fear of what other people will say about them and the second is the fear of what they will say if it doesn't work! I wrote this book for the person who is in a constant dilemma over what they see and want, and what they must do to obtain it. *It is written to conquer fears:* fear of what others think or say; fear of not wanting to admit our own failures; fear of the unknown; fear of speaking or having to get out of a COMFORT zone. This book will make fear fun! It will transform your fear into something like an exciting ride in a racecar. The ride may be scary at first, but the thrill of success will exhilarate you. I also wrote this book to answer questions about a person's ability to go from the ordinary ranks of money and moderate freedom, to the extraordinary heights that we read about: Fifty thousand dollars a month, not a year! Paying cash for the car! Wearing the Rolex, because the Patek Philipe is in the shop so the diamonds can be cleaned. This book is for the person who is tired of living in the *"What is"* mode of life and wants to move into the *"WHAT IF"* mode of possibility thinking.

Will this book erase all your fears? It is possible, but remember, fears are like butterflies in the stomach — while you can't chase them away, you can make them fly in formation. This book will show you how, and explain to you why you swallowed the butterflies in the first place. Once your fears are marching in order, you can carefully choose what company, product and system you wish to use. Then you can succeed beyond your dreams. Any number of avenues will work for you if you are ready and know the principles for success in Network Marketing.

3 x 5 CARD

I once lived in the world of
"What is."
Now I flourish in the positive world of
"WHAT IF!"
(*Show someone a picture of your dream today.*)

Psychological Principle #2
LEADERS KNOW
THERE IS MORE THAN ONE
PATHWAY TO SUCCESS.

I had a friend once tell me, "There are many ways to skin a cat." Then with a wily smile, he mumbled some real wisdom, "The cat hates all of them!"

You have already decided to be in Network Marketing, so I am not going to sell you on the merits of this mode of getting rich. Your ability to succeed will depend on how you overcome your biggest obstacle, *your belief system:* your belief in yourself, the industry, the company, the product(s), other people, and in the possibility of obtaining your dreams.

The systems for obtaining wealth through duplication are academic. They will work. It IS a numbers game. The speed in which you achieve financial success is the only question, and that speed depends upon *whether you <u>act</u> on what you learn.* You may need help getting out of the COMFORT zone into the FEAR zone.

⁄⁄ Important Note ⦥

I said financial success. Other successes attainable in the Network Marketing arena are public speaking, personal development, self-esteem and so on. You must decide what you are after and the level of expertise you want to attain in order to be a winner in business as well as the game of life.

Why do we want to enter the FEAR zone? Because that is where the money is; the money to live in the world of the successful and the fulfillment of helping others to arrive there with you.

One of the premier consultants to the *Wealth Building Industry* today is Jim Adams. Retired comfortably out of Network Marketing, Jim suggests that "Courage is not the absence of fear, but it is working in spite of the fear. Courage is moving forward through fear." Jim continues, "...people put themselves down because they are afraid to talk to strangers. Leaders must show new distributors that moving through the fear is the key to financial success. Few fears are ever conquered, but all fears can be managed."

Since 1991 I have spent time on the beaches of Cape Cod, Malibu, St. Thomas, Waikiki, and Martha's Vineyard. I have visited Jamaica, Puerto Rico, San Carlos, Virginia Beach, St. Croix, Vancouver Island, and Haiti. I have seen New York, Chicago, Mexico City and Montreal. I have toured London and Toronto. I have driven the Florida Keys. I have appreciated the snow on the Canadian and Colorado Rockies, the Alaskan glaciers, and the top of Mt. Popocatépetl in Mexico. I was able to travel to these places *while* I was pursuing my financial goals *not because* I had achieved them. That is what the FEAR zone has to offer! The FEAR zone is not a bad place to spend your next five years. Getting you in the seat of the racecar is the hardest part. Once you are in, you are on your way!

Psychological Principle #3
SUCCESS IS EARNED
IN THE FEAR ZONE,
NOT THE COMFORT ZONE.

Network Marketing *is* for everyone. However, not everyone is for Network Marketing. A career in engineering, dentistry or dental hygiene may not be for you. I cannot do engineering. There is no way. Math and I are planets apart. I cannot stand the mixture of teeth and drills — no dentistry for me. I cannot conceive of picking a piece of bologna out of someone's teeth — it would not happen. No career in dental hygiene for me! I admire those who can do it and I am glad they do it, but these three professions are not for me! They are not for everyone.

Network Marketing is a method of selling. It is a duplicable program that allows anyone to find his niche, and earn the same incomes or more than the dentist, the engineer, or the hygienist.

Network Marketing/MLM is the finest form of entrepreneurship on earth. It is pure possibility. It crosses all boundaries of skill or talent. Anyone with a desire to achieve and strong work ethics is able to compete in this arena. The opportunity is based on averages. The odds can be tilted to move faster or slower; nevertheless, the outcome will be the same for anyone who gets involved, works hard, has a positive attitude, and *never quits*. It simply follows the *Universal Law of Cause and Effect*.

Are you ready for your dreams to come true? If the answer is yes, then let us enter the FEAR zone together. In the upcoming principles, we will discuss why we have fears and why they continue to hold us back. Even more importantly, we will turn your fears around and make them your allies. Fears can become our friends. It may even surprise you to know that fears can bring about a great deal of fun and profit! *Another reason I wrote this book is to make money.*

3 x 5 CARD

*I once lived in a world called
the "COMFORT zone."
Now I thrive in the adventure world of
the "FEAR zone!"
(Do something that terrifies you, today!)*

Psychological Principle #4
IT'S OKAY
TO SELL SOMETHING
TO ANYONE!

We are all entrepreneurs. If that is difficult for you to understand, then the principles of this book will help you the most. It's *okay* to make and talk about making money. It's a good thing for you and I to sell to each other things that will bring benefit and enjoyment into our lives. It's *okay* to make a profit! And it's *okay* for us to sell to friends, family, and even strangers! It's *okay* to say what you want, and then go after it. At first people may laugh at you, but when you are holding your loved one in a tender embrace overlooking Diamond Head in Waikiki, or you are on top of the Pyramids of Teotihuacán in Mexico, you will have the last laugh. Let me give you an example.

In 1989, my wife and I owned a sewing factory that went belly up. My neighbor, a jovial man named Al, suggested that I apply for a job at a large hardware store where he was working. It was a nice gesture on Al's part, but I was not interested in the least bit! I was going to get into Network Marketing. It was not clear to me where or what I would be doing, but I had read the stories and I was going for it! Al watched with interest as we struggled in the early months. My wife, Gabi tried one company for about a month. She was doing well (on paper). One day, Al knocked on the door and held up the front page of a newspaper showing the CEO of her company being arrested. Al thought it was pretty funny, but my wife was devastated. Al continued to invite me to come down and fill out the application at the hardware store. All the while Al kept laughing. When Gabi and I began realizing our dreams through Network Marketing we moved away from the old neighborhood. The next time we thought about Al was five years later. We were celebrating our twentieth anniversary at the Ritz Carlton Hotel on Amelia Island, Florida, relaxing by the pool overlooking the beach, when I sleepily asked Gabi if she remembered Al. She didn't answer. I wondered if Al was still working at the hardware store. I think I fell asleep before Gabi said anything. Anyway, I hope Al is doing okay. And if he is reading this, I doubt he is laughing anymore! P.S. Al, don't send me an application for the hardware store. The answer is still, *"No!"*

I tell this story to make two important points about Al. First, he always complained about not having money, and second, we asked him to join us, and he said "NO!" It was *okay* to offer Al the business. It was *okay* that he said "NO!" It was *okay* that he laughed. Really! Our job is to offer the opportunity. That's all. People will either say, "Yes" or "No" and that's *okay*! What is NOT *okay*, is to get into the business and not offer anything to anyone. If Al had accepted the opportunity, it would have been *okay*. It would have been *okay* to *"Make money from a sale to Al!"* Just as it would have been *okay* to eat in a friend's ice cream parlor, and not get a discount. It would have been *okay* for your friend to make a profit on the ice cream purchased from his store.

Another fear people have is the stigma of "getting rich off their friends." Don't fret about it. It won't happen. Remember, your friends are probably broke already, so you "aren't gonna get rich off 'em!" In fact, you won't get rich off your enemies or family members either. You will get rich the same way all people get rich, by working smart and hard.

/& Important Note &

Those people who claim that you only have to work smarter, not harder, are not very smart! You must work smart and hard!

Work smart by leveraging your time and talent; and even more important, work smarter by helping others make money first. And finally, it's *OKAY* to offer the opportunity for success to your friends and family. Really! It's *okay!*

If you genuinely want something, it's *okay* to ask friends, neighbors, relatives, angels or the universe! The question is what do *you* really want?

Many people are confused; they don't know whether they *truly* desire more money or subconsciously want something else from owning a Network Marketing distributorship. More than 80% of the people I have worked with needed recognition, association, and camaraderie more than they desired money. Their *real* needs are manifested through their attendance at meetings and social activities. They enjoy the personal development aspect, but do not actively offer the opportunity to others. Money is not their primary motivator. I have friends that get emotional when they talk about peripheral benefits they have gained in Network Marketing. I have friends who get emotional when they talk about money! Guess which ones have the money? Remember, money is *okay*. A friend of mine says money is tainted. It is only tainted if it "taint yours, and it taint mine!"

Our main goal here is to provide you with an effective tool that helps you conquer your fear of "selling something to anyone" and helps you bring positive results to your business.

Ninety percent of success is overcoming fears. Many people find public speaking to be one of those major fears (something I can relate to). I had to overcome the fear of public speaking many years ago. By overcoming fears and turning your weaknesses into strengths, you'll discover the true blessings of success.

My career as a professional speaker and writer for the past twenty years has given me the opportunity to travel and reach thousands of people. It has allowed me to fulfill my life's mission of changing peoples' lives for the better. It is in my blood. I was fortunate to have been employed as an executive by two Network Marketing companies. My wife and I have also worked together and developed multimillion-dollar distributorships with each company.

⚜ Important Note ⚜

We developed each distributorship separately and in consecutive order. You cannot develop two successfully at the same time.

We have been very successful. We live a wonderful lifestyle. At the time of this writing, Gabi and I have just returned from a marvelous seven-day getaway in Jamaica! (No problem Mon!) We had many of our top leaders there with us. In my twelve-year history with Network Marketing, I have seen many rewards, such as, time and money freedom, and the thrill of seeing other people's dreams come true. We know that you *can* build for yourselves a strong residual income, and do it in your spare time, because we have done it!

My biggest drive in life, however, is the next public speaking opportunity. It allows me to make a positive change in someone's life from the platform. It is a wonderful job and a dynamic challenge. I love my mission in life. So why write a book? *Why would anyone write a book for his competition except to make money?* We all enjoy making money. I admit I do, but I also love seeing people succeed. It is a great reward if you can help someone get ahead in some way. The truth is I love my work and I love getting paid for doing what I do.

It is interesting to read some creative answers network marketing experts have developed to explain why they are selling their books (containing the true secrets about building a successful business) to their competitors. I have found it easier to say, "I sell books to make money. I do it for a living. I sell vitamins, pet shampoo, and other great products. *Wannabuysum?*"

My *primary* profession for the last twenty years has been as a trainer and motivator. My *part-time* profession is marketing a great line of products through the MLM *sales technique.*

Serious wealth builders should concentrate *on their system*, which works for *their own organization* and should not strive to confuse other distributorship lines. What I mean by "confuse" is simply this. I listened to a tape produced by a man who has reputedly earned more than one million dollars-a-month; he says, "You will never understand wealth in Network Marketing until you understand depth." I have a book from a different gentleman who says, "You never worry about depth. Go wide, wide, wide!" So what does the new person do? He gets confused. *To avoid more confusion we are just going to talk about YOU, and the "mind-set" you will need to succeed. There is no system offered here.*

The WBI (*Wealth Building Industry*) arena offers an even playing field for all participants. It allows ordinary people to become extraordinary. This book was written about *what you must become to get what you want* from the WBI. Many systems of success are available for you to use. Who knows? You may even develop your own success system. However, developing the "mind-set" for success is a must.

3 x 5 CARD

> *Everyone wants to buy from me.*
> *They want to buy something*
> *that will enrich their lives*
> *and bring them happiness.*
> *I will show them my inventory*
> *of opportunities.*
> *(Ask someone to buy from you today.)*

Psychological Principle #5
KNOW WHAT YOU ARE REALLY SELLING!

Let's start in MLM 201. (MLM 101 was the book that described illegal pyramids and all that other stuff!)

Have you ever seen a poor network marketer? Oops! Maybe you are one! Well, if you are, you are not alone. Ninety-eight percent start out thinking they are poor. Would you like to know which ones stay poor? The ones that sell vitamins. Oh yes, or the ones that sell soap and detergent, or the ones that sell water filters or make-up. Let's not forget the "poor" network marketers that sell long distance service or insurance policies. Am I missing anyone? So who gets rich? We know there are some rich people selling all these things. Why are some rich and some busted? The money is in the banks of the people who can learn to lead and get into the *"people business"* by selling the most important product of all –*OPPORTUNITY FOR WEALTH!*

Let me clarify this point. The late Cavett Robert tells a story about a convention he attended in Pittsburgh, Pennsylvania. It was a gathering of the American Steel Manufacturers' Association and the featured speaker for the day was the Executive Vice President of U.S. Steel Corporation. Cavett said he expected a tall broad shouldered man to approach the podium. After all, he was the number one salesman in the world "with more sales flowing across his desk than any man alive." To Cavett's surprise, a "little baggy-pants fella with some buckets" walked up the center aisle of the convention hall and placed the wooden buckets on the stage. Cavett said he thought it was the janitor and that it was a heck-of-a-time to be mopping the floors. The speaker then asked, "Whatever happened to the old oak buckets? They're in the Smithsonian Institute. What I am most concerned with, is what happened to the oak bucket companies? They're bankrupt! You know why? *For too long they thought they were in the bucket business. They forgot they were in the 'people business'!*" He went on in his speech to identify industries that were suffering because they forgot this important fact. "The railroads are bankrupt because for too long they thought they were in the railroad business, instead of realizing they were in the business of solving people's transportation problems. I don't care what you do, banking, real estate, or manufacturing battle ships. If you fail to understand that your job is solving people's problems, you won't be in business long."

Leaders know what they are selling. We are selling the opportunity for people to become somebody — to become important, successful, rich, happy, and free. *We are in the people business*, and we believe in the unbridled potential of the human spirit. People ask, "If I only had a chance..." Well, we sell that chance. Those who don't make it in our industry are selling vitamins, soap, water filters, long distance service, or a myriad of other great products. In 98 percent of these cases, when someone focuses on product sales, rather than developing people, their business ceases to exist. Like the oak bucket companies, they are out of business within a year or two.

Do you know that most Network Marketing product sales are done within a distributor's first 90 days in the business? This is when they are most excited about the products and opportunity. After that, the actual sales a distributor will generate will not alter much over the years. Although their income can skyrocket, it does so only if the excitement stays up enough to keep that distributor prospecting. The products alone cannot do that. The desire to share the opportunity can keep you pumped up, and you never get tired of sharing it if it is working. You can earn linear income through the movement of products, but *only sharing the opportunity for wealth can drive duplication wide and deep.* So, are you in the product sales business, or are you in the people business? Are you selling vitamins, soap or long distance service? Or *are you selling the opportunity?* Guess what the rich distributors do? You've got it! They sell both effectively, but are only driven by one. Which one will make you some cash? Which one can make you rich? (Hint: one opens a door, and one opens a bank.)

3 x 5 CARD

I am not in the bucket business;
I am in the people business.
(Touch someone today:
give a handshake using both hands,
or give a warm hug.)

Leaders know how to make big money in Network Marketing.

We often refer to Network Marketing or MLM as an industry. Realize that the title is not exactly accurate. The word "industry" means: *"the commercial production of goods or services."*

We all work in, buy from and sell to many different industries. All of the Network Marketing/MLM and Direct Selling companies do not belong to an organized "industry." *Network Marketing/MLM is a SALES TECHNIQUE, not an industry.*

As I mentioned previously, there is a large group of entrepreneurs that cater to companies marketing their products through Network Marketing/MLM. Some examples are: legal groups who offer consulting services; writers who produce specific training programs and books; companies who produce tapes or put on conventions; and speakers like myself, who specialize in training for companies using the MLM *sales technique.* Another way to look at it is that there is an auto industry that produces cars, a health and nutrition industry that produces vitamins. Some companies in these industries market with the *sales technique* called MLM. MLM is actually a sales method and the *"industry"* of MLM, can only be correctly defined as *the people and companies who provide books, tapes and consulting to companies who use the MLM sales methods.*

As a professional speaker and trainer, my job has been to teach people how to be more successful, not only in their job, but also in their personal life. In Network Marketing seminars, I teach distributors how to get positive results in their businesses and overcome fears, not just from a stand-point of motivation, but from a point of learned experience — experience gained from being both a distributor, and a Network Marketing Entrepreneur. (A Network Marketing Entrepreneur such as myself, or a publication like "Upline®" magazine, does something which universally supports the direct selling companies. Both provide a service or a product for profit. Both would technically be the Network Marketing or MLM *industry*.)

There is an industry of successful leaders, who use systems that can produce residual wealth for those who desire it. They vend opportunity. They sell methodology, and a "mind-set" for building wealth. We call this great "industry" that creates wealthy people the *Wealth Building Industry* (WBI). It is young, and not well formed, but it is growing each year.

If you are seeking wealth by helping others to obtain it, you are in the *Wealth Building Industry* (WBI). If you were looking for vitamins, you would look to the health and nutrition industry. You could choose to purchase from an MLM-oriented company, or through a more conventional way, such as at a drugstore.

If you are looking for a residual income, some options may be to investigate recording a C.D., tape or a record, or you could write a book, or sell insurance. These possibilities *can* develop a residual income. (Assuming of course you can sing or sell!) Or you can go to the MLM industry, as I did, to learn. Here, you can buy the products to learn the methodology to build "walk-away income." I spent four years reading material from this industry between the years of 1981, and 1984. I did not join any particular company, but read and researched material written about Network Marketing and MLM *sales techniques*.

The product you choose to sell and make money with, may be vitamins because of their extreme high daily consumption. So you would choose a company within the health and nutrition industry that has an MLM sales plan. Notice here that we are talking about two industries. *First* you must become a vendor of what these industries produce (in this case vitamins); *second*, you must become a vendor of what the true WBI industry produces: the opportunity for wealth!

So, are you getting it yet? To be an owner of a product of any industry, you must pay for the product you want. The same is true to obtain wealth building knowledge. You must pay. Nevertheless, if your desire is to get paid from any industry, you must learn to sell their products, whether they are vitamins, or wealth building knowledge and methodology. The only things WBI, produces as an industry, are *leadership* and *wealth building opportunity*! In order for you to become wealthy in the WBI, *you must learn to sell dreams and leadership.*

3 x 5 CARD

*I am a master of
the MLM sales technique.
I sell wealth building information.
I am helping people to be free and rich!
(Ask someone if they would like
to be "rich" today.)*

We are the Vendors of Dreams and Leadership!

To better understand how you can be successful in vending (selling) dreams and leadership, let's draw some mental pictures. First imagine a picture of the car salesperson. Can you see a salesperson of fine cars, which cost $100,000 or more, and the salesperson on a small used car lot? Both people could be successful in their respective jobs. The results in terms of personal income could be very wide. Wealth can come to both of them if they succeed to *own, DUPLICATE* and *expand* in franchises or multiple dealerships. This of course would require learning about dealerships, laws, management, leadership and so on. People who have obtained big dollars in either the new or used car business did it with duplication and multiplication. There is no other way.

So it is with the *Wealth Building Industry*. Many people who sell vitamins for a *linear commission* (exchanging time for money) think they are going be rich some day. In reality if they do not learn to build dealerships, train managers and develop leaders, then wealth will never happen. Granted, they may earn some good money, and even find some time freedom, but the true *WBI players who become rich, do so by becoming sharp, talented leaders of people.*

So what does a Dream Vendor look like?

How do you feel about yourself? Are you willing to make a dramatic change in your life? Is your mind right for success? Do you like yourself? How do you look? Can you change your appearance, or learn to love yourself, just the way you are? Can you read, talk, and conduct meetings? Can you motivate others? Do you need to take a public speaking course? Could you benefit from a speed-reading seminar? Have you learned to be enthusiastic? Energetic? Do you have the confidence to be rich, to be a leader?

I am sorry if I may be dashing the dreams of the person who feels they can have the goodies and not pay the price. Nevertheless, the examples of that happening are as rare as for me to record a "Top Ten" hit. (I sing like a frog with the flu.)

Also, beware of the snake-oil salesman. The person who stands up and tells you "Ah isn't oll theat smart, wha ah caint ayven say theyem big wards, but hayek, ahs made may a kabillion pazazools layast week!" Trust me...theys know what theys are a doin...I mean doing!

So, first things first. YOU must define YOUR success. Do you want to be a top salesperson for a great line of products, and maybe even have some sales people in your group that you get paid for managing? Or is your definition of success a long-term solid income that would be considered WEALTH? What do you really want? What are you ready to give up and sacrifice? You must define what you are willing to do. I heard it said once, that it is best you become a millionaire before you get the money, and then you will get to keep the money. Are you a "mental millionaire"? Does your heart accept that you are worthy of such success?

I met one woman who said all she wanted was $100,000 a year. That was all! She had a mediocre job. She could not remember the last book she had read. She did not keep her appearance up well. She liked to watch television when she could have been working. She did not listen to tapes much, and she thought she was underpaid. She was willing to join our company if she could JUST get up to $100,000 a year. I asked her how much that was per week. She said she didn't know. I asked her if she would settle for $1,900 a week or so (which is about $100,000 per year). She said, "That's a start, but I really want the $100,000 a year." She just did not get the picture. She was the sad person who was, in reality, content, and liked to wish a lot. This would be the person, who will commit to very little and want you to do all the real work. The woman did not know exactly what she had to give or do to get the $100,000. In rough figures, it would probably translate into approximately 80 to 85 successful distributors doing about $2,000 per month in sales —not at all an unreasonable goal.

Remember, you must be like first class athletes, who know *exactly* what they want. They know to the 100th of a second, the time they must run to break a record. The same is true for massive success. You must know exactly what you want, and precisely what you will give to get it.

I am reminded of the story of a drunk laying on a park bench, offering his half-full bottle of cheap wine in salute to a passing limousine, *"There, except for me, go I!"* Then he took a swig, and saluted again, "Here's to the holidays, all 365 of 'em!" A commitment to leadership is a powerful life changing commitment. For those who successfully do it and pay the price, it is fulfilling beyond imagination. It is privately annoying for winners to hear the whining of those who want the achievement, but are not willing to pay the price.

Often, successful people get bitten by the lazy or unsuccessful people. I remember as a youth, my father stopped our car on the way to church one morning to help a small black dog that was caught in a fence. Before the ordeal of releasing the trapped animal was over, my dad needed 11 stitches. So it is with people. If you don't first learn to lead, you will be bitten. I am confident the dogcatcher would not have met the same fate as my dad did. A dogcatcher is prepared to handle such situations.

Again, what are you willing to pay to see your dreams come true? Have you made your decision as to what you want? Max DePree states so eloquently, *"The first responsibility of a leader is to define reality."* Some two thousand years ago a doctor quoted a leader to say, "For which of you, intending to build a tower, sitteth not down first, and counteth the cost, whether he have sufficient to finish it?" It is my hope that in defining what leadership is to you, it is not discouraging, but encouraging. I hope it is time you stand to say, *"My time has come, and I will have it. No one will deny me. I will have it all because I will pay whatever price it takes. I define leadership. I am a leader!"*

3 x 5 CARD

> *I am a Vendor of Dreams.*
> *I sell a plan to fulfill hope.*
> *I am looking for sharp talented people.*
> *(Compliment a sharp person today!)*

I CAN CHANGE AND GET BETTER, BECAUSE I AM A LEADER.

A leader "leads people." He will lead by *attraction*, not by *promotion*. It is a fundamental stepping stone to fulfill-ment. If he cannot help, inspire, and lift people, he cannot lead, whether he considers money an issue or not. Jesus was a great leader, whom we do not associate with money. To our best knowledge, he owned perhaps sandals, a white or purple robe, and maybe a donkey. Yet he could rally more than 5,000 people to hear his sermons. The reason is he was lost in helping other people, believing in their abil-ity to improve themselves, and in serving others.

Leadership, whether noble or ignoble, requires inspiring people, preferably for good causes.

In 1522, Francisco de Aguilar wrote of Cortez, "(He) gave us very good talks, leading us to believe that each of us would be a Count or a Duke, and one of the titled. With this he transformed us from lambs into lions, and we went out against that large army without fear." "Went out" they did, conquering the mighty Aztec nation at odds of more than ten-to-one against them. The key here is helping people to go out "without fear!"

Great Leaders are Passionate! *Do you understand? PASSIONATE!* I mean *really, incredibly, overwhelmingly PASSIONATE!* In our quest for leadership, we must understand that passion transcends talent. I have heard some poor public speakers drive a crowd to frenzy and excitement through pure passion for what they believe in. As a WBI leader, you had better obtain a passion and a fire to bring success to others. It has been said of one great historical leader, "(his men) could not understand what (he) said, but no matter, they would have followed him cheerfully barefoot, and without provisions." That leader was Napoleon.

3 x 5 CARD

> *I am passionate! I talk with passion;*
> *I walk with passion; I think passionately;*
> *and I share my passion*
> *for success and happiness*
> *with anyone that will listen!*
> *(Raise your voice five times today,*
> *but not in anger.)*

One man in our industry is a terrific example of leadership through passion. He had been an insurance salesman, and felt that one certain type of insurance was "ripping off the American consumer." He developed his own company, and organized a startup group of less than ninety people. His vocabulary was rough and he had a heavy Georgian accent. He gave talks that were similar to the locker-room motivation talks that he learned in his first career as a coach for high school sports. His passion was overwhelming. Within ten years his leadership drove his fledgling company against all odds to the pinnacle of success. Battling one of the most powerful industries in America, he revolutionized insurance selling and contributed greatly to the possibility thinking of the WBI opportunity. It was his ability to use passion, to cause other people to perform that determined the outcome of his company's *multibillion-dollar* success story.

Another principle we must understand is that leadership can be for better or for worse. Hitler was a superb leader, and had a powerful group of leaders with him. Leadership skills have no conscience. Honorable leadership means "worthy" leadership, freedom leadership, based on honesty, openness, and integrity. Unfortunately, there is no value given to leadership skills. They will work for good or bad people. This is a major cause of failure in the Wealth Building Industry. *People sometimes follow the wrong leader.*

One of the best examples of wrong leadership is the person who is telling you what to do, but *has not earned the right to lead.* To lead first means to learn to follow, and to be a student. Instead of following a proven system, the *"fakes,"* or *"wannabes,"* have not earned the right to develop systems. They do not yet understand the nature, culture, nor demographics of an organization in a specific region, and they break away thinking they are above those who have blazed the trail before them. They are the people with all of the answers, but none of the money.

THE FAKE DIAMOND!

Generally these leaders (whom I will label as Zirconias) do not do well, and their organizations falter. The problem is the mistaken aura of leadership that the new distributors see. They follow the Zirconia's guise of leadership, not realizing the Zirconia is fulfilling a personal selfish ambition to shortcut the process and gain admiration. Zirconias are not willing to pay the price, and they are not showing the skill and art of apprenticeship. A true leader first pays the price as a good follower, apprentice, helper, and student. One who fails to take the time to learn and follow, is like the brain surgeon who shortcuts classes and cheats on tests during the important college years. Would you want such a person operating inside your head? (Zirconias try to get into your head every day, but with words instead of a knife.)

I am reminded of the historical story of one of the most intelligent men that ever lived. He was Leonardo da Vinci, an artist, an engineer, a sculptor, a community leader, and a visionary. At the age of eighteen he was placed to learn from the great artist Andrea del Verocchio. After a time as a student, Leonardo surpassed his teacher. This discouraged Andrea to the point of stopping his art. I believe this is what a good student should do: learn until he surpasses the skills of his teachers. Then he is truly a qualified teacher. Leadership begins by first learning to follow. (I guess it's too bad Andrea did not sponsor Leonardo at five or seven percent! Whoa! I don't think he would have quit!)

I remember when I first took boxing instructions from the Dutch light heavyweight champion, Hank Jensen. I thought he would put me into the ring and let me start banging and boxing away. I was disappointed because for weeks he had me pound on a bag and run laps to get in shape. After my first three-minute round, I realized we should have ran more and stayed on the bag longer!

A Leader is patient. A true leader understands that leadership is a practiced art form, and not an inherent trait. A leader continues to learn his trade even after he is leading. The stories of the new sales leader upstaging the veteran professional are proverbial. Here is another one I heard. I believe it is a variation of a story credited to Art Holtz. A sales leader took a new recruit out to talk to people and learn to close. Each time the leader attempted a sale he was shut down. Each time the "greenie" attempted a sale, he crossed himself religiously, and then succeeded. The leader had been making the best of the situation by saying it was good to learn how to handle rejection, and was praising the "greenie's" sales with beginners' luck. At one point, hiding his frustration, the leader said, "You must be deeply religious, right?" The new recruit responded, "Yes sir. I am." The leader continued, "Do you think if I crossed myself like you do, I would close more sales?" "No sir," was the reply. "Why is that? Is it because I am not very spiritual?" asked the leader. Then came the moment of learning that all leaders must face from time to time. "No sir. You don't close, because you're a lousy closer!"

A leader seeks knowledge. A leader always seeks greater wisdom. A leader strives to use intelligence. If there is no wise application of the material we have studied, there is no intelligence! In other words, a person may be good, but good for nothing!

Leadership requires action of a productive nature. The Zirconia will read and teach. He will be active in doing things, but not productive. A Zirconia is always working on the computer, reading and studying, but seldom sponsoring in any productive quantity, either on his front level, or to give away the leads to his organization. Zirconias see themselves above all this, too good for doing the basics, not realizing that it is the example they set that is of real benefit to new people. Remember, Napoleon, Alexander and his father Phillip were great generals because they were on the battlefield leading. Christopher Columbus did not send the Pinta, the Niña and the Santa Maria; he went with them as the pilot. When we think of Teddy Roosevelt, we envision him in Cuba in 1898, charging up San Juan Hill with the "Rough Riders." We think of Winston Churchill's stern face as an adult, but as a young officer in the army, we see him in 1899, charging under fire, at Boers in South Africa.

So now, when we envision Mary Kathleen Wagner, (Mary Kay), Forest Shaklee, Rich DeVoss and Jay Van Andel, we see them in great offices presiding over their huge companies. We fail to imagine Art Williams or Mark Hughes out on the "firing line" doing the basics, feeling the frustrations and pain of success. Yet, that's exactly what all of these modern-day marketing geniuses did.

In my early days of MLM sales, I had often been afraid to go back to the basics, and only did so when I was forced to because a group expected it. Only when gaining maturity in leadership will you realize you are only as good as your last story. *You must continue to do the basics when no one expects you to.* Dan McCormick, 17 years in multi-level marketing, millionaire many times over, thinks like an athlete, "Every single day I must execute the basics, whether I am earning $500 a month or $60,000 a month. You just can't afford to deviate from them." Only then are you truly respected. The work you do when you are alone thunders in the ears of the followers so loudly that they rarely hear the Zirconia's rhetoric.

A Zirconia has excuses in his declaration of leadership, but *a true leader has results.* A Zirconia will tell you what he is going to do, while the leader points out what has been accomplished. Zirconias say *"if,"* Leaders say *"when." Leaders are accountable, not excusable.*

As a leader, you will have people who will reject you. *You cannot be a leader and please everyone.* If you are pleasing everyone, you are not a leader, you are an enabler. While it may stroke your ego, money and respect will evade you. We fear and love leaders. Just as your child will fear you and love you, so it is with true leadership. People will fear you because you challenge them to go where they have never been. You must become vulnerable to those you lead. They fear you, because you push them, you don't pamper them. They will love you because you will never let them go alone into the dark. You will tell them what to expect, because you have been there before. You will play no favorites as the Zirconias do, but you will reward justly to all the deserving. A leader understands that leadership means to be known for better, and for worse. Often the most loved leaders of history, including religious history, are also, at the time of their leadership, the most hated. It is a price that must be paid. Are you up to it?

> I heard two talking the other day
> I was surprised at what I heard them say
> "He's a snake in the grass," said Riff to Sill
> "Of him everyone's had their fill"
> "Not I," said Sill, "I know him not
> Ah, but I'll bet he's a stupid clot"
> "Yes," said Riff, "he's as dumb as a stiff."
> And he seethed and he wretched within
> "All that he'll touch, will soon be corrupt
> To him pure virtue is sin"
> "He's a worldly waste, and I say to all
> Part company without any haste"
> And so they went along their way
> And they scorned and they scratched as they went
> And I pondered as they walked and thought as they talked
> Is harm their only intent?
> For I knew in my heart as I felt it smart
> It was I they were talking of
> So I fell to my knees and begged, "Father please,
> Bless me once again from above
> Of all the blessings Thou has blessed me with
> Bless me these are them I can love."

One of my first lessons in leadership, came when I was a teenager, and I heard others talking about me. My friend's parents were speaking badly about me, and I overheard it through a door. I withheld anger, and turned it to pain and penned the poem you just read. To this day I read it to remind myself that for the fun, money, respect and appreciation that leadership offers, there is a price that we must pay.

A leader does not give pain. A leader BEARS pain!

A leader understands love.

A leader says, *"I love you."* The leader learns in his apprenticeship, to tell parents, brothers, sisters and family members that they are bonded by love. They then learn to appreciate things and the world they live in. They graduate learning to love mentors, and heroes. They gain true friendships of both genders. They learn to tell them *"I love you"* and mean it. Then, finally, they move into the higher realm of service, in which they can love strangers, and even enemies. Will Rogers said in his own unique way, *"The Bible says to love your enemies, but just for practice, why don't you try it on your friends?!"*

3 x 5 CARD

> *I love those who do not love me.*
> *They may not understand life as well as I do,*
> *so I am compassionate and patient.*
> *I understand the higher laws*
> *of service and forgiveness.*
> *(Ask for forgiveness, and*
> *forgive someone of something today.)*

Those who enter the noble profession of vending dreams, those true networkers who understand leadership, are not the people who earn by deception. There will always be the occasional Zirconia who is a scoundrel, front-loading everyone he knows, and then moving on to the next deal. These are not leaders. They are opportunists. In their own lives, they are miserable. My wife calls them *"trash flies."* They prey on the good people, often taking most of their savings with promises that are doomed. Why are they doomed? They are doomed because these losers will never be there to train and help their people succeed. They will move on, looking for someone else's savings. This is bad for business. They are bad leaders, understanding only those principles of leadership that skirt responsibility and vulnerability. It is like a cake box that has a lovely picture depicting the finished cake, but only contains the sugar.

I was scuba diving in Jamaica with a good friend from Texas named Kevin Kutter. Kevin and I were following our underwater guide, a Jamaican named Errol. He was a kind man, with an endearing smile, and he knew the waters well. He took us to a lovely dive spot called, "The Nursery." It is so named because of the friendliness of the fish. They knew Errol, and swarmed around him. It was beautiful to behold. The water was clear, and the weightlessness of diving allowed us to literally "fly" and "float." Kevin and I were ecstatic and enjoying the event. It was one of our greatest dives. Then Errol opened a plastic bag full of bread. It instantly clouded the water and the fish began a feeding frenzy. Errol would put pieces of the bread between his lips, and the juvenile Sergeant Majors (a beautiful yellow fish with black stripes) would nip at it, giving us an amazing close up view of the event. When the bread was about gone, he opened the bag, and held it open. The frenzy so excited the young inexperienced fish, that eventually one entered the bag, eating as though it had won an eating spree at a Las Vegas buffet. Then, Errol closed the bag. When the fish realized we had trapped it, its movement stopped. It panicked for a few moments, but within seconds it fell into a stupor, and became motionless. We examined it for a short time, and then released it. Stunned and dazed, it slowly swam away. Its delight had become a nightmare. All that it had hoped for was free food, and in reality it had entered a trap. We had lured and caught it simply for our amusement and interest, and then let it go to never be seen again. Did it learn something? Who can tell, but I would bet that if we could have marked its tail, we would never see that fish again.

Kevin and I discussed the event later on the boat. Bad leaders, the Zirconias, will use the same entrapments on unsuspecting people, luring them into a world of possibility, surrounding them with dreams and hopes of a better lifestyle without paying the price. They then release them without ever having taught the basic principles of leadership necessary to "have it all" and "keep it all." Dazed and confused, they swim away uninterested in dreaming anymore. Zirconias who do this show poor leadership and give our WBI a bad name and cause people to "over-learn."

A cat will jump onto a hot stove once, but will never do it again. However, the cat will probably never jump on a cold stove either. It will be totally out of the "stove-jumping" business. So it is with innocent and unsuspecting prospects —after one bad Zirconia, they call MLM a scam. The saddest fact however, is that even real Diamonds become fake in the eyes of those whom Zirconias have cheated out of their dreams.

3 x 5 CARD

> *I have determined the price of success;*
> *I know what I must do;*
> *and I do it every hour of every day.*
> *It is not my business;*
> *it is my way of life.*
> *(Tell someone about a good book you read*
> *and ask him to read it.)*

Psychological Principle #7
A TRUE LEADER IS HONORABLE AND FAITHFUL.

A leader is a pillar of honor, and firm in his resolve on noble issues. He understands the higher laws of service, and he is always a leader. Day in and day out he is who he says he is. The "fake it till you make it" syndrome is no more than an outward trapping. It is not the inner personality.

A true leader will dress and look successful in life prior to financial achievement, but never lie about what he has and earns. I recall, often, while we were climbing the ladder of achievement, my wife and I would go to the finest stores, and examine the clothes. We would memorize the labels of the best garments and shoes, and then drive to the second-hand stores and painstakingly go through the garments to find quality clothing. I always wore expensive Italian shoes, high-quality suits and first-rate shirts. (Forget the ties, they're always yucky in second-hand stores.) I purchased them with gratitude in my heart that someone else was thoughtful enough to give up these garments to a second-hand store so another person could dress first-class for a fraction of the cost.

When I am doing a seminar on dressing for success, I always wear clothing from a second-hand store. Generally I pay between fifteen and twenty-five dollars for something, then another thirty-five dollars for altering and cleaning.

I tell the audience the actual value of what I am wearing, using current retail prices. It is usually around five hundred to a thousand dollars, had I bought it all new. I ask them, "How do I look?" They laugh and give me some whistles and applause. I tell them how much I enjoy being able to shop at the best stores and buy the best clothes. Then I tell the truth, "I can shop where I want, and I do, but these I am wearing this day, are clothes bought, with pride and dignity, in a second-hand store." If that is where one must begin, then the leader will begin there. *Humility is not an embarrassment. It is a virtue that a true leader must deal with.* He cannot teach it unless he understands it.

3 x 5 CARD

I am not concerned with status.
It is fleeting and transparent.
I am who I am and I display a natural class,
and a confident demeanor.
Humility is a private virtue to me.
(Stop by a second-hand store today
and buy something.
They need your support,
and you need the experience.)

Great leaders are empathetic before they are sympathetic. Leaders understand the nobility of a humble beginning, and the need to climb above their circumstances. *Leaders are not victims of circumstance. They are creators of it.*

Once one accepts the mantle of "leadership," he has to accept that he must forever improve his mind. If he cannot accept and tattoo this on his psyche, he must settle for being a good follower. *A teacher teaches. A GREAT teacher is a student.* School is never out for the professional. Never! Dan McCormick says, "There are no masters of MLM, even the best are trying to get better at listening, learning, doing meetings, and teaching. Whatever it is, there are no masters, only learners." A leader is a reader. He is a bookworm and a "tape"worm. A leader should be a speed-reader. Speed-reading is a learned skill that one must begin working on the day one commits to success. One can check out books and tapes from a local library. There are continuing education courses that can be taken. If you want to be a leader, then you must stay ahead of those who will follow and you must catch others who are ahead if you want to be competitive in the industry. Leaders mark up books. I generally buy two books — one to tear up, and one to read. Before I had the money for two, I would again go to the second-hand bookstores and pay pennies on the dollar for great material. Even now we still prowl the antique stores. Recently, my wife and I bought seventy-two books from an antique store for two-hundred-fifty dollars — one set of fifty-four classics, and a complete set of Will and Ariel Durant's "*The Story of Civilization.*"

The classic look of the antique books adorns my library beautifully, but the sublime nuggets of wisdom I read will adorn my mind for the rest of my time on this planet.

A leader reads psychology and pop-psychology, religion and philosophy, history, biography, and autobiography. A leader of people studies peoples' lives and motivation. A leader reads everything pertinent to his profession; he goes beyond reading, seeking to understand and absorb what he sees.

The Zirconia, on the other hand, reads occasionally. He will use the same interesting point repeatedly, or make a hobby of a particular book or philosophy.

A Zirconia leader will always seek to be in front of the room, but will not have production numbers to have earned the right. He will often qualify himself by some achievement of the past. In today's business pace, there is no place for those who cannot *"walk the talk."*

A true leader, is an honorable "doer" of the work, a tireless example full of enthusiasm and energy. He is there when you are down, and seems to sense such times intuitively. Such leadership is rare, and such a leader knows how rare he is. His noble issues can often be painful, and if left to linger, can delay success.

Everything seemed to be against us when we began our career in the WBI. We were living in Phoenix, Arizona. Our family business had closed its doors, and we were in a financial crisis. As we all know, when it rains, it deluges. My father passed away, and I did not have money to attend the funeral in Washington State. A friend loaned me a credit card to rent a car (my car would not make the 1,700 mile trip.) I loaded some bread in the car, and laced a one-gallon jug of cheap lemonade with liquid vitamins. After a loving embrace with my family, I set out for the long drive from Phoenix to Spokane, Washington. My children gave me a large plastic water jug full of pennies they had been saving for "Dis-lee-land." (My 2-yr. old daughter could not pronounce it properly, but she wanted to go there someday.) As I drove, I would roll the pennies from the jug. Just as I would get twenty-six rolls counted, my car would be out of gas, so I would stop for fuel and make the station attendant mad by paying with rolled pennies. Counting the pennies while driving was difficult, but it got worse as a massive snowstorm blanketed the entire western half the country. I owned a beautiful hunting knife that was a gift to me from my father-in-law. I took it along with hopes that my brother would purchase it, so I would have gas money to get home. He did. Between the tears and the snow, on the way to bury my father, I reached a low ebb in my life. I was broke, and embarrassed, and felt that I had let my family, myself, and worse, my own father, down.

I was shocked when apparently my father spoke to me from the grave. I entered a gas station somewhere in Utah or Idaho, and paid for my gas with my pennies. A small voice inside me said, "Ask them about your business." I resisted. How disrespectful! What kind of son would push his business at a time like this? I felt ashamed to even think about it. Again it seemed that my dad spoke to me, "You have a wife and five children at home. You will be five or six days. You must keep working. A funeral only lasts a couple of hours. Keep working son. You must take care of my daughter-in-law, and my grandchildren."

As I placed the wrapped pennies on the counter, and signed them, truck drivers stood impatiently behind me. Fighting the tears back I said in a timid voice, *"Would you like to know how to earn some extra money in your spare time?"* Neither the clerk, nor the truckers said a word; they just stared at me silently. Perhaps they all saw my misery and pain, or they thought I was making a joke. There were no takers, not even a "No!" The clerk handed me a receipt, and I left. Did I sponsor anyone? NO. Did I learn something? YES, a great truth. You can make excuses; you can let others make excuses for you; you can let circumstances get in the way; or you can do what is necessary (and expected) for YOU to become successful.

At home, my wife was just as hurt at the loss of my dad, but she had to tend to our five children. The second evening I was gone, one child rolled off a bunk bed and split open her forehead. She was rushed to a hospital emergency room to have stitches. Another child with a severe bladder infection was rushed to the doctor the next morning.

My wife had scheduled business presentations the entire day with one of our new distributors who was very excited and showing much promise. Now she had to decide. Should she keep the appointments or take care of the children's needs. She was torn. With me being out of town, she knew there was no one to take her place in giving these presentations. The new distributor was so excited. He was on fire! He would probably have understood if she had cancelled, but his momentum would have been lost. She knew he had to succeed in this business! Alone, it was time to make a leadership decision, a decision for our future. It was a turning point in her life. She opted for calling her sister-in-law to take care of the children and she went on her appointments. It was a very difficult decision to make, but she remembered hearing that during harvest time a farmer does little else than bring in the crops, and he must make many sacrifices. It is the same in your business. During the first year, you do most of your planting, and sometimes *you* must make many sacrifices.

The children do not recall the incident. They do, however, love their lifestyle and the opportunity it affords them. For many years they have had parents who work at home and are accessible just about any time. Once, the phone was shut off because we couldn't afford to pay the bill. Now, it is not unusual for me to be a thousand miles away on a stage and have my cellphone ring, "Daddy, can I have some ice cream?" Now I am always accessible to my children, because we can afford it.

The sacrifices we make on the path to obtaining our dreams are temporary, but the rewards are permanent.

Being an honorable "doer" of the work, and working with a firm resolve to see your quest through to the end under any circumstances, brings a sense of joy and fulfillment few will ever know. It's not easy, but it's worth it beyond your dreams.

3 x 5 CARD

*I am a creator of circumstance,
never a victim of it. I am a pillar of honor. I
stand nobly, unafraid to advance my cause.
(Stand up for something today, anything.)*

A LEADER IS OFTEN
ALONE IN HIS QUEST

Often joy and appreciation surround a leader; he never appears to be alone in his quest. A leader is generally left alone during adversity. Aloneness is a crucible that melts down the Zirconia, but brings out the best in the "true-action" person.

A true leader must question all advice, and listen intently, even to the least of those whom they lead. This can be difficult. It can give a person the perception that the leader does not trust them, but it is necessary. There is a great temptation to accept too readily the advice of those close to you. I once phoned the Vice President of my company with a great idea. It was logical and well thought out. I knew that, if it was carried out, it would succeed. Nevertheless, to my surprise, he suggested that I try it out, and then call him with the results. I was, at first, hurt, but then I realized that his leadership required him to qualify the idea first. Since it was my idea ... guess who had to perform?

A leader is often alone. Time he spends with people in a meeting or at a convention is wonderful, but often there are ten or twenty hours of travel time for the leader just to make the two-hour meeting.

A leader can be alone in his opinion. Sometimes it may seem that heaven and earth are against him. Yet if his cause is noble and right, if there is a chance he can persuade and prevail, it is his obligation to fight and use every honorable means necessary to bring about his victory. However, if the timing is not right, *if some of the leader's ideas are not accepted, he bears no malice, and he accepts it.* He changes his opinion if necessary, and he supports the general cause he is involved in. For example, when a leader loses a political race, he congratulates the winner, and goes back to work for his own and his followers' ideals.

A Zirconia will scowl if you do not accept his idea. He takes it as a personal rejection. He decides that something is wrong with others, because they did not accept his idea. Often he can be so upset that he spreads venom and rumors, picking away at other people. Some will quit over misunderstood rejection.

I met a couple who had joined our company with great excitement. They had tremendous growth at first, but they received a box of products which *they* thought were of poor quality. They made some suggestions to the company on how to fix the problem. The company did not see a problem with the product. The rejection tormented them for months. A year later, I saw them at a national convention, and they were still angry over the situation. They had done nothing to build their business all that time and concluded they would not build it until the company fixed the problem.

A Zirconia can even seek to find vengeance if he feels bad enough. There is no place in WBI for revenge, anger, or hatred. This is a business built on relationships of the positive kind. Some people however, have the kind of attitude that lights up a room when they leave it! You know the kind I am talking about — people who could make you wish we had retroactive birth control! If you have a streak in you that sometimes tells you to "get even," this business is not for you.

Leaders don't chase the snake!

I remember an incident that occurred during my youth. My church took a group of young people to the desert for a hotdog roast. They were around sixteen years of age. One young woman wandered into some brush and was bitten by a rattlesnake. The boys chased the snake for several minutes, until they found it and killed it. Only then did they rush the young woman for medical attention. She lost her foot due to infection. The doctor said that time was of the essence, and had they rushed her in immediately, she would have been okay. Where was the leader, who *alone*, acting without guile, could have taken the stricken young woman for help while the others sought revenge? Zirconias will chase the snake. True leaders do not.

Remember, Paul Revere rode *alone*, Patrick Henry stood *alone*, Jesus stood before Pilate *alone*, Napoleon and Paul died *alone*, and Helen Keller was *alone* in her dark and silent world for years, waiting to be liberated. Anne Sullivan required that she and Helen be locked away *alone* to succeed in bringing Helen out of her darkness into the light of leadership. Helen would eventually learn several languages. How many can we speak?

In December of 1996 Jean Dominique Bauby collapsed. He was a world famous editor of the fashion magazine, *Elle*. Waking twenty days later from a coma, Jean found himself paralyzed and only able to blink his left eye. He was only 43 years old. Jean had lived a beautiful, rich and successful life. He worked in a world of high fashion, lace, limousines and beautiful people. He had a beautiful wife and two lovely children. Now he was alone like a butterfly trapped in a diving bell. People would attend to him, for he was not able to help himself in any way. But he could blink his left eye. When someone would point to a letter, he would blink, and they would write it down. Letter by letter he sedulously created words, then sentences, then paragraphs, and eventually a book. Called *The Diving Bell and the Butterfly*, the title signifies the subject and his new physical reality — a brilliant mind trapped in a paralyzed body. He was not a Zirconia. He was a Leader. In his loneliness, he wrote of the travel adventures within the depths of his mind.

"My diving bell becomes less oppressive, and my mind takes flight like a butterfly. There is so much to do. You can wander off in space, or in time, set out for Tierra del Fuego, or King Arthur's court." He continued, "You can visit the woman you love, slide down beside her and stroke her still-sleeping face. You can build castles in Spain, steal the Golden Fleece, discover Atlantis, realize your childhood dreams and adult ambitions."

His magnificence was realized in his infirmity. I shutter to think of how I would have reacted under such a condition. Jean was a leader, not a Zirconia. In his loneliness, he continued to lead. They published his book, and two weeks later he died. His nobility remains as an inspiration to all who would lead.

So what does the WBI leader learn from this incredible story? Jean did not let anything in life stop him from his quest. I don't believe he knew his own death was impending, but even if he did, he performed. He performed nobly and honorably. I see Zirconias every day that are willing to give up or quit for the worst of reasons. *A leader sees obstacles as something to stand on so that he can see the goal more clearly.* Zirconias use any excuse to give up, or at best, fail to act. *A leader performs alone, when no one is there to cheer.* He goes for it even when no assistance is available. He seeks friends and support; he wants association and community, but if he must, he will work alone in the dark. He recognizes the importance of the mission, and he never forgets it. Ronald Reagan's father taught him to *"decide what is important, and then never forget that it is important!"*

Some of us need the loneliness to discover the giant inside. Some leaders handle the aloneness better, because they have had experience with it, and they recognize it. Perhaps Helen Keller and Jean Dominique Bauby learned it after the challenge presented itself. How much stronger are we who can *learn* from the experiences of others, unlike an animal, which is bound only by genetic coding and personal experience.

I learned of loneliness and leadership at a young age, that leadership hides in all of us, waiting to be released if we will go for it in life. My father was a leader, but like Jean Bauby's infirmity, alcoholism trapped him in a different kind of diving bell. We always felt that he had tremendous possibility, that his body housed a sleeping giant. Still, in our dysfunctional home life, the leadership was always just beneath the surface. Unable to break the shackles of his vice, he retreated to a miserable camp trailer in the middle of Phoenix, Arizona. Surrounded by a million people, he was waiting to die. His own family resided all around him but we seldom embarrassed him with a visit. Honestly, we were uncomfortable to be with him.

I was once talking to him about being lonely, and I said I understood what it meant to be lonely. He said I would never understand loneliness until I was surrounded by a million people (including my own family), and no one knew or cared that I was there.

He had considered suicide, but in this, he exemplified leadership. In later years, he said it was all he thought about every day. One day he made a choice between life and death. He chose life, cleaned himself up, and asked people for help. He accepted an invitation from his oldest son, my brother Ira, and he moved away from the misery he had lived in for so long. In time he met a lovely lady, they fell in love and got married. He became involved in community and church service. He became a blessing to his children and grandchildren. At age seventy he joined Alcoholics Anonymous, and was clean for seven years before he died peacefully. At the time of his death, he was a pillar of leadership in his community. More than three hundred people attended his funeral. I was amazed at the size of the crowd.

So where is leadership? When is it time to become the giant within? Only you can assess your life and decide. Is there a silent giant inside you waiting to be set free? Or will you need a paralyzing tragedy to bring out the best you have?

The Zirconia leader sees difficulty and challenges as his enemy, not his stepping stones. To the Zirconia everyone is a threat in some way. A true leader sees only one threat, one challenge to success, and that is his own "mind-set" — his own opinion of what he can or cannot do. That is the challenge for the true leader.

3 x 5 CARD

> *I am blessed.*
> *(Buy and read*
> *"The Diving Bell and the Butterfly,"*
> *by Jean Dominique Bauby.*
> *Do it today!)*

LEADERS ONLY HAVE ONE ENEMY TO OVERCOME - THEMSELVES.

I read a story about an explorer in Africa who had his camp visited by a native dressed in nothing but a spear and face paint. He was the tribal leader of his clan. As the native rummaged through the camp, the explorer and members of his camp tried to ignore him, so as to not scare him into aggression. One man was shaving, using a sharp knife and a mirror attached to a tree. The native, curious why a man would have a knife to his throat approached and watched. Adjusting his angle to see what the man was looking at, the native saw his own reflection, and quickly speared the mirror, shattering the glass. When asked what had happened, he said he had seen an enemy in war dress, and he had killed the enemy to protect the man with the knife. He did not realize that *he* was the enemy he was fighting. It was his own reflection that had scared him.

In most cases, we are our own worst enemies, and often our biggest fear is not what others will do to us, but what we are doing to ourselves.

One book I would love to write is *"You're Right!"* The book title will be *"You're Right!"* Chapter One, *"You're Right!"* Chapter Two, *"You're Right!"* Leaders realize what Henry Ford said was very accurate. Whatever a person thinks, is the way it is to him. *If you believe you can do something, you're right. If you believe you can't, you're right.* If you feel others hold you back, you're right. If you believe nothing can hold you back, you're right. You're right, you're right, you're right!

⚹ Important Note ⚹

Zirconias can be identified as those people who see others as some type of threat. Leaders will be identified by seeing others as healthy competition.

3 x 5 CARD

> *You're Right!*
> *(List 10 reasons for each:*
> *why you succeed or*
> *fail at anything.)*

Zirconias find the reasons why things will not work. Leaders find out why they will. Zirconias say, "This town is saturated, burned out on MLM sales, and you can't build here." Leaders say, "This town knows about MLM, and just needs to see my opportunity!" Zirconias are the "would-be" leaders who don't have time when you need them, but if you asked them to count dollar bills, and keep all they count, they would be free twenty-four hours a day!

Who is holding you back? According to Henry Ford, we hold ourselves back. We are our own worst enemy. Knowing why we hold ourselves back however, is important. But it is more important to know what to do to change inactivity to action, and activity to productivity. So let's go back to the fundamental reasons why we usually do not live up to the standards we expect others to live by. Humans are, by nature, negative.

Now, if you are one of those people who think you are just as happy as a "bug-in-a-rug" all the time, and you are astounded by this statement, be patient. I think you will agree with me that you need to work on keeping yourself happy, not sad. I have never met the person who tries to depress himself. It just doesn't happen, unless you are unbalanced and on medication. Let's face the truth. We are, by nature, negative. There are no doctors who treat "chronic happy disorder." Yet there are thousands of professionals who treat depression. Treatment of depression today is, in fact, an industry!

Perhaps the reason is this. We know that our personalities are almost completely formed by the age of six or seven.

If we analyze the forming time of whom and what we are, we can discover some very interesting things. For nine months, we are carried around in mommy, floating, warm, protected and sleeping. Then in our first experience in the air-breathing world, we are held upside-down in public, while a stranger wearing a mask slaps us on the butt. Our mothers are watching, and condoning the act. Next, our flesh is cut at the life-support system and tied in a knot –and we are not even offered the option of an "innie," or an "outie." We are manhandled, somewhat like a bag of potatoes, for several minutes, washed, weighed, poked and probed and finally given to a warm lady that smells familiar. We are calmed down and fed, with no explanation of why we had to endure this rude awakening. What an interesting way to come into this glorious experience we call life.

So here we are, after nine months of bliss, thrust into ten minutes of misery and terror. Then it is over, and our bliss begins again, better than before. New tastes, new smells and touchy-huggy things are all around us. Every waking moment is a discovery. We go for swinging rides up and down while strangers say "WHEEE!" (Whatever that means) We do not have to worry about eating or sleeping. If we want food, we cry. If we want to be held, we "coo." It is all so automatic, so convenient, soooo wonderful. It continues for about nine more months of our life (only ten bad minutes out of eighteen months, not bad.)

Yet somewhere in this life of bliss, I personally believe we have our first conscious talk with ourselves. A talk that is somewhat like a conversation two pigs were having at the trough one day. The farmer had just emptied another lovely feast of slop into the feeding bin. With a soupy mixture of rotten veggie bits, and garbage, the pigs were in swine heaven. Overweight, cared-for and fed constantly, one pig stopped and stared into the blue for a long moment. His "being" was so content, he felt a completeness of self, and a pure feeling of gratification, but questioned his purpose. His companion was sucking down the slop like it would end tomorrow. The pondering porky stared into yonder for a moment, then said to his companion, "Have you ever wondered why farmer Brown is so good to us?"

But back to our wonderful warm first months of living. During this blissful time as infants, we could do no wrong. We could spit on people, barf on them, wet on their laps, and they would laugh and tell us how cute we were.

Indeed, we could do no wrong. Then, we took our first step…and reached for the vase. That's when it all began. "Don't touch that!" "Put that down!" "Leave that alone!" "Don't walk in the street!" "Stop, wait, sit, stand" and so on. During this time, which does not last six months — it lasts up to *nine years* — we learn all the "N" apostrophe "T" words. "*Don't* go there." "You *shouldn't* do that." "*Couldn't, wouldn't, won't* and *can't*." Some have estimated that a child will hear variations of the negative word "no" more than eighty thousand times by the age of ten, while they will hear the word "yes" only five thousand times. If you add up all the negative words associated with "no" delivered to the subconscious mind, the damage to the child is staggering. Is it any wonder that the human race is primarily negative?

Society has shown that a child reared in a loving home will generally be more positive than a child raised in a dysfunctional setting. By repeatedly telling a child he is worthless and no good, the child will be left with a low self-esteem, and usually be more inclined to committing a crime. Because each of us had different levels of positive influence, we are all on different levels of ability to be positive.

Our "negative nature" began even before we were born. We know that the subconscious mind remembers and believes everything it receives. Though we may forget something, we file it in the brain. Our retrieval system is the conscious mind (CM), our everyday thinking mind which questions, doubts or rejects ideas. The subconscious mind (SCM) places no value on the information it receives and it accepts everything as truth. For example, a hypnotist will tell a hypnotized person something that is warm is in fact cold. That person will genuinely believe the item is cold. In their hypnotic state, the CM is bypassed with information that is contrary to reality, but accepted as a truth to the SCM. So if you say to a child, "You're rotten, you're rotten, you're rotten," the chances are very good that, in time, the child's conscious mind weakens its resolve and will accept the information. The subconscious has already accepted the information to be true and filed (stored) it. The great disaster is that we never learn this until we are adults. We need a program that teaches the unmarried teens how to properly talk to their future children. They need to learn to say to a child who is about to walk off a porch, "Walk this way, sweetheart," instead of "Don't go there!" Since this simple understanding is not imparted in a pre-parenting format, the negativity curse passes from generation to generation. Now don't be too hard on Mom. She did the best she could.

Whatever positive information, on a balance scale with whatever negative input that was innocently placed in the deep recesses of your SCM, determines your ability to be positive.

As adolescents, we began to question the input, and frequently, even fight back. When someone told us we were dumb, or ugly, our SCM accepted the information, but our CM started defending itself. "I'm not dumb," (and, remembering what we learned in Sunday school.) "God didn't make no junk!" This positive information, though it is derived from our own defensive thinking, also imprints on our SCM. These positive statements, recorded in the SCM, are good input, but they are terribly slow coming, and can do little to offset the eighty-thousand-plus negatives implanted during the formative years. Whew! Are you getting all of this? Do you see now why some of us are, by nature, grumpier than others?

Although changing the way we are mentally may seem hopeless, it is possible. However, it will usually take a lifetime to do. An example, is the Grandma or Grandpa who is so warm and wonderful. A lifetime of tempering and learning can positively manifest itself in the twilight years. It may have taken sixty-five years to change what was imprinted in ten years.

So tell me. What happens when you say to someone, "You can have it all, you can be a leader." Consciously you get an "Okay, let's get started!" Subconsciously, neither of you hears the eighty thousand reasons why it won't work.

We cannot remember that we once held titles like "terrible two's" and "He's a three-year-old!" These titles were given to us by our moms and dads or others who didn't realize the indelible imprint that was being made on our subconscious mind. And the more damaging the title may have been, the faster our conscious mind dropped it from memory, into the recesses of the subconscious mind where it festered and formed a nature of negativity that haunts us for a lifetime. "You're worthless!" "Can't you do anything right?" "Will you ever get it right?" Words like dumb, stupid, wrong, worthless, brat, ugly, different, lazy, and all the "N'T" words are all there, holding us back.

The defense mounted by the CM has been admirable, but it is time to root out the real problem, and forever render it ineffective. We must overcome negativity in order to soar to the limits of our true potential.

3 x 5 CARD

> *I rarely say "If," I say "when."*
> *I rarely say "I," I say "we."*
> *I rarely say any "n" apostrophe "t" words.*
> *(Write down all the words*
> *you can think of that end in*
> *"n" apostrophe "t",*
> *then throw the paper away.)*

Psychological Principle #10
THE SUBCONSCIOUS MIND REMEMBERS EVERYTHING!

It is the memory recorded in the subconscious mind that will make your dreams come true, or keep you from them. It will reflect in your eyes, in your undertones of speech, and in your aura.

People have toiled for months, perhaps years, trying to build a large, successful WBI business only to realize, "It isn't happening." Often they are told the reason is the "aura" of negativity they project to others. This may very well be true. If you are just going through the motions with a CM (conscious mind), that is hoping and wanting things to happen, it is quite possible that your true core belief or SCM (subconscious mind) is still not accepting the possibility of true wealth and success in your life. Though your conscious mind may have forgotten much of the unpleasant past, the subconscious mind has not! People often rightfully blame this point for their failures. You are a product of your upbringing. You may be overlooking the fact that what is holding you back can also be the secret to your success.

If the SCM remembers everything, and we are a reflection of our core belief, then let's fill it up with what we want to be! That's right! Fill it up with what we can do, what we are, what we want to be and do. Let's fill it with all the good we have learned and possibilities that lay at our feet. This is done through affirmations. An affirmation is a positive statement made in the present tense. When read and/or verbalized daily with power and conviction, it overrides the negative input that our SCM has accepted over the years. We so overlook affirmations that it is ludicrous. Negative affirmations messed up our heads in the first place. This proves that they work! So let's get it fixed through positive affirmations!

Once our SCM is fixed, we can sell anything to anyone without fear. We can excitedly approach anybody. We can speak in public, manage business affairs, and create a large and successful wealth building business.

So, we know our parents and others lambasted us with eighty thousand bad or negative affirmations. Like a balancing scale, we need to add eighty-one thousand positive affirmations to turn it all around. Sounds simple, right? It is. The logistics are the hard part. How do we get eighty-one thousand positive comments into our SCM?

We can begin three things today that will positively re-program our SCM:

1) *Turn all incoming information into a positive.*

2) *Personally inject voluminous positive
    affirmations to yourself.*

3) *Associate exclusively with positive people.*

Let's talk about each one.

FIRST, how do we turn all incoming information into a positive? Start by realizing what a wonderful world we live in. Realize that objects, which seem to get in the way of our success, are there to help us, not hinder us. Challenges build character and strength. Look at difficulties as stepping stones, not stumbling blocks.

Have you ever noticed how a group of ants will get by something? They do not hesitate at any obstacle. They just move over, around, or if necessary through it. If you could speak the chemical language that ants speak, what would they think of you if you said, "I don't want to get by that rock!" Most likely, you would be laughed out of the colony, or eaten for lunch. The relentless little ant can teach us volumes about persistence without complaint. It will surmount any object (hindrance) that is in its path. It is just something you deal with, without malice, care or concern. Ants don't wake up each day and say, "Boy, am I tired. I think I'll sleep in." They just set out to take care of the day. They decide what must be done, and get it done. To an ant, cutting a piece out of a leaf, and carrying it home is important enough to die for. They will do their job no matter what. Jim Rohn once said, "If you're looking for me, come to California, look for the highest mountain you can find. Look for me there. I'll be waving from the top…or dead on the side." WBI leaders just get "it" done. If you need to ask what "it" is, see your sponsor. Leaders are positive about the challenges! Always seeking the positive in everything they have to deal with, they will tell you that "even a broken clock is right twice a day." (They can really drive you nuts!)

A leader grows strong in adversity. Leaders see the abstract benefits that Zirconias are blinded to. A snake's venom is not a poison; it is a substance used to make antivenom in case a snake bites someone. It is also used in research for relieving joint ailments. A dam does not impede the river's flow, it allows generators to create "light" and provides lakes and beaches for recreation. *Leaders flourish in adversity.*

Leaders are able to find the useable nature of every situation. Honorable leaders will seek the positive in everything they see. No act of service is so small that it should go unnoticed. They are often so positive they border on the ridiculous. Leaders will seek the good from anything that confronts them. They believe everything has a positive use in our world. Lord Bacon said, "Even a hair casts its shadow."

Lincoln said, "Hardships are too precious to lose." He was so right. We must remember that precious stones are chipped, then ground, and polished to become brilliant gemstones. Iron must be melted, and beaten to become steel. Great oak trees weather the heavy winds to build the fiber to survive ages. *So WBI leaders will achieve greatness only by serving in the trenches and learning to develop through earned effort.*

Too often we forget that adversity carries the seeds of opportunity. Can you think of any success that wasn't born from a challenge? Success means needs are fulfilled, challenges are met, difficulties are overcome and most importantly, leaders are created.

J.C. Penney said, *"I never feel sorry for poor boys. The children of wealth deserve sympathy; too often they are starved for incentive to create success for themselves."*

Obstacles that cause disappointment must be seen as positive steps in the ladder to dignity and greatness. When a challenge arises, say to your SCM, "YES!" Raise your fist in the air, and bring it down quickly as you declare, "YES!" It may sound strange for you to do this, but *unless you change your point of view on strength from adversity, leadership will always be just outside your grasp.*

I was in a print shop with a fellow distributor named Ray shortly after we got started in MLM. We had ordered four hundred copies of fliers we were going to hand out. Since it takes about ten minutes to run them off, we decided to pitch the printer, since he was our captive audience. Upon asking him if he would be interested in a Network Marketing business opportunity, he began a tirade of how bad he felt MLM sales were, and how only losers would participate in such a deal. He went on, and on, telling stories of woe and misery that he supposedly had heard about. On and on he talked, never asking any questions. Indeed, it was he who had us as the captive audience. Eventually the copy machine stopped, and we paid and walked outside. I was dazed. My friend jumped in the air, pulling down his fisted arm and rapidly pumping it like he was pulling a bell rope. He exclaimed, "YES! YES! YES!" I yelled,

"What?" He said, "That man gave us enough negativity to last us for the rest of the month!"

A leader will flourish in the adversities of life. He will see them as positive events, as challenges or calls to bring out the BEST from within. "YES!"

The result of this action will start the change of attitude and begin the bombardment of positive data rolling into the SCM. This is what we need in bringing about the defeat of our negativity.

It is easier to ACT into a new way of thinking, than it is to THINK into a new way of acting. Leaders ACT.

3 x 5 CARD

*It is easier to act
into a new way of thinking,
than it is to think into
a new way of acting.
(Today, act like you just won
a million dollars,
but you cannot tell anyone.)*

I really like the story of the African native related earlier. I believe that when you have read this book several times, you will have speared the enemy within, in order to create the new, fearless you. The new you is a gift to yourself, to all that know you, truly a gift to the world. You see, you could be anywhere right now, but you are here, working on self-improvement. There are so few in the world today that care about improving themselves, that when someone does make an effort, it inspires everyone around him.

The transformation journey will not stop there however, the crowning event will be acting on what you have read, and sharing it with others. Remember, a sunrise cannot fully be appreciated, unless you can reach out to someone and exclaim, "Look!!"

I wonder if in the quiet moments, you say to yourself, "I'm pretty sharp. Why can't I figure it all out and make it work? Why can't I have it all instead of just pieces and bits? A lot of people who aren't as smart as I *think I am* have what I want. What am I missing that they are not?"

I am not saying each of you reading this is feeling this way and if you are not, if you are just as happy as a pocket protector salesman in a IBM® lunchroom at noon on pay-day, that's okay. There is someone out there you can reach out to with this information, someone that needs to hear from you.

It is important however that you realize that beginning today, you can change and be whoever you wish to be. If you want to be different, that can happen as quick as you can say the phrase, "I am different. Today it all starts anew for me. Today I am a new person." *This is true even if you feel like you are a loser.*

I've got to tell you, I personally like the word loser. There is a sense of humor about it, because to me it describes people who choose to lose. There are hundreds of stories of poor people who never had poverty thinking. They worked hard and amounted to something. But losers never do. Someone once told me a loser is someone who's nicest towels say "Motel 6®" on them. Losers are negative by nature, and sincerely desire two things — to stay negative, and have you remain with them. A loser answers his phone by yelling, "Check's in the mail."

People will always be down, or get down. That's life. It is what you do to address your situation that really matters. It is how long you stay down that matters. If you stay down in a boxing match more than the count of ten, you concede victory to your opponent. That is the fact. It is the rule, the rule of life we must all live by. Winners get down, and they go down, but they rise again and again if necessary, and fight. And do winners make mistakes? Of course they do, but they will correct them and go on. Losers will run and justify.

3 x 5 CARD

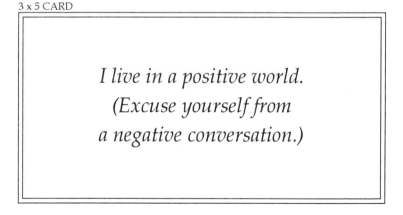

I live in a positive world.
(Excuse yourself from
a negative conversation.)

In the year 1618, King James I appointed a man Lord High Chancellor, perhaps the highest appointment in the British realm. The man had earned the right. He had other titles, Baron, Viscount. He had been knighted in 1603 and had served the crown as Solicitor General to the throne, and sat as a council board member to the King's affairs. Then much to the surprise of all of England and Europe, he was charged with over 20 counts of bribery. For 10 days the world waited and watched for his rebuttal. The world waited to hear how unjust accusations would falter before this servant of the people. But it didn't happen. Instead came the humble reply, "My Lords, it is my act, My hand, My heart; I beseech your lordships to be merciful to a broken reed." He confessed. He had done wrong. He was the greatest lawyer of the British realm. He was wealthy. He could have weaseled out of it. But he chose to win, and win rightly. He lost his seat in Parliament. He was banished from the courts. He was sentenced to prison. He was fined 40,000 Pounds! An unbelievable fortune in 1620. What disgrace! But was it a destruction of a life? No! Because this candidate for being a loser, chose to win.

He corrected what he could, put his broken life back together, and served his fellow man. Today we revere Lord Francis Bacon, not a criminal, but as a Great philosopher and statesman. Today we enjoy, and indeed relish his great literary works, such as his sublime essays covering such modern subjects as truth, death, adversity, parenting, marriage, living single, envy, love and boldness. He wrote of goodness, nature, nobility and troubles. He lectured on atheism, religion, and superstition. He wrote on counseling, wisdom, innovation and friendship. He wrote of health, riches, ambition and fortune. But he also wrote on honor, reputation and judicature.

Besides Lord Bacon's Essays, we have the treasures of his literary skills in the works of the History of Henry VIII, The Wisdom of the Ancients, and Advancement of learning. He opened the door for the first time since the dark ages for practical philosophy to be understood and accepted over pure metaphysical speculation.

Today, we quote him daily: "Some books are to be tasted, others to be swallowed, and some few to be chewed and digested." Or this, "Knowledge is power." And one last one you may have heard, "The sun, though it passes through dirty places, yet it remains as pure as before."

Perhaps at times we see ourselves as losers. If for some reason you have a setback, or have had them in the past, whether they were real or imagined, legitimate or unfounded, today they will disappear. Any memories of those events that cause us to think less of ourselves will only be remembered as stepping stones to our success.

Whatever our real or imagined handicaps are in life, they will never keep us from what we are destined to do if we are determined.

Even in deafness, greatness is achieved. How can a deaf man write music? Yet, as we often stand or cry when we hear the beautiful refrains of Beethoven's Eighth and Ninth symphonies, we seldom reflect on the fact that he was tortuously deaf when he composed them. His teacher was

Hayden; his model, Mozart, yet he would surpass these genius-level composers in deafness and write what we all know as the "Ode to Joy," which when heard, transcends the human experience.

If we pause for a moment, and consider what the man might have done had he not been deaf, we cheat both Beethoven and ourselves of what greatness is; for in his lifetime he left us 138 works including 9 symphonies, 7 concertos, 1 septet, 2 sextets, 3 quintets, 16 quartets, 48 sonatas, 8 piano trios, 1 full opera, and 2 masses. My point concerning greatness is this: *if his hearing had been better, he would have produced less, not more!!* It is in trial that people who choose to succeed win. Only losers seek the easy paths.

And today is a day of choice for you. Are you ready for it? Are you ready to win? Are you in tune to be the superstar you sense within you but have not yet witnessed? I believe today is the day you win. This is the hour, the minute you choose to succeed. To choose success over failure, happiness over despair, wealth over poverty, freedom over bondage, love over hate, smiles over frowns, forward over backward, enlightenment over darkness, kindness over rudeness, agreement over disagreement. Today is the day we seek cheer over gloom, knowledge over ignorance, and wisdom over foolery. Now is the time to have action over re-action, books instead of television, and health over sickness. From now on it will be harmony over strife, strength over weakness, and courage over fear.

I heard it once said that when we cease to grow we begin to die. Well, we are going to grow. Another person told me that it is mandatory to grow old, but it is optional to grow up! I like that!

You have chosen to read this book and grow. That means you have thrown yourself into the "living," not the "dying" category. And it does not matter economically where you are coming from. Both rich and poor are the same in many ways. For example neither rich nor poor can determine the weather. Much to my disappointment, I discovered it rains on the wealthy too. As we enter into the realm of affirmations, a world that can take you to your dreams in life, let me also say you are going to sleep less, but enjoy it more. I believe you are going to get more money. I believe as a result of these affirmations, you are going to have a better lifestyle, and your outlook on life will improve. I know people are going to like you better, and you are going to like people more too. Sounds amazing, doesn't it? Well, there is more. I believe you are going to get offers and opportunities. You are going to laugh more, cry more and your self-esteem will soar upward to new heights. I've seen it happen many times. I believe you will find new self-confidence and as a result and benefit of acting on what you read in this book, you will become more ambitious, more industrious, even be more courageous.

You might be asking, "How can I be sure that some dramatic change will take place for the better?" Well, it is simple to understand. The principles have been around forever. Most people do not know how to properly use and believe affirmations, even though the principle is as old as dirt. A saying that was attributed to Henry David Thoreau stated, "We must walk consciously only part way toward our goal, then leap in the dark toward our success." Now is our time to leap, even though the advice comes from a long time ago. A better example you might relate to is the quote, "Would yee both eat your cake and have your cake?" First heard near the end of the 1500's. Today we say, "You can't have your cake and eat it too." It is very old advice. But do we save our cake (or money), or do we eat it every single week until there is too much month at the end of the money? In the 1300's, it was Geoffrey Chaucer who said "Doeth with your own thing, right as you list," or, as we know it today, "Do your own thing." And, believe it or not, it was Ben Franklin who coined the phrase, "Hang in there" back in the 1700's. The wisdom has always been there. We just need a funnel to somehow pour it into our souls so we can internalize and utilize it.

The *SECOND* thing we need to do, is begin injecting positive affirmations into our own mind, by reading them, writing them, and hearing them. Over and over an unending flow of positive information about us must settle in our conscious and subconscious minds.

I wrote a booklet of positive affirmations that I felt I needed to read each day to get ahead. Thousands of booklets have been circulated since its first publication. Each affirmation has an explanation that helps clarify its meaning. Let me share them with you. It is important to copy down and internalize the affirmations. (There is no need to copy the explanations.)

Here are the affirmations (and accompanying explanations) I wrote and use daily:

I am truly lucky.
I have the world
and all its opportunities at my feet.
The world owes me nothing,
but the world will
deny me nothing.

One hundred and twenty-five thousand children were born into countries of famine and starvation for me to be born in the splendid conditions I live in. No starvation, no nakedness, no misery.

I am unique in all the world.
My value is more than
the earth I live on.
I am a wonder of the universe.
I am unique in all of God's
creations.
I am programmed to endure
and flourish in adversity.

My body is made up of seventy billion cells. Each tiny cell has the computer memory to reproduce my entire being and keep me alive each moment. My tear ducts function flawlessly twenty four hours a day. My heart beats automatically. All of this incredible body that I take for granted, functions day in and day out without conscious thought. All of this in one tiny cell. One cell could reproduce itself into another me. A computer which could match the functions of my cell, would take up an entire city block in microchip technology and still be less effective and functional than my tiny cell.

I totally control what enters and remains in my mind. Those I love and accept are permitted to influence me positively. Negativity in any form has no place here.

When Victor Frankl was imprisoned in Auschwitz during the Second World War, he said that his captors, the Nazis could deprive him of his liberty, but they could not take away his freedom. Although it is easier to say than do, we must realize we are in total control of our mind. We can think in any manner we wish. Our problems begin when we believe what others say. In the very second that we affirm that we alone determine who can enter our minds and influence us, we begin to accelerate the journey towards the success we dream about.

I flourish in adversity. I run to challenges and champion a great cause, my cause. I need no permission granted to me to know how important I am, and how much I am needed.

When I lift weights I become strong. The winds build the strength of the mighty oak. The largest sunflowers reach for light above the rest, or remain small. Iron is beaten and heated to be made into steel. Stones are chiseled to become polished. Soldiers are verbally driven to become disciplined and effective. The fastest runners run the most. Why would I seek greatness in any other way than the manner set forth by the universe?

I absolutely amaze myself.
I am incredible.
Greatness requires me to see you
as absolutely amazing.
You are incredible.
I can achieve anything.
You can achieve anything.
We, together,
can achieve anything, faster.

A tiny fly can fly! I cannot. A spider can build a home in a day. I cannot. Everything living on the earth is superior to me in some way. I am superior to every living thing on the planet in some way. I can lure and capture the fly and I can slay the spider. My greatness lies in me, not in what others think of me, for that would be a fleeting and false greatness. Only what I think and believe matters. I respect myself as superior to all that is living in some ways and less than all that lives in other ways.

Failures and setbacks in life
are my workbench.
They are my stepping stool
for success.
I do not regret them.
They move me forward;
teach me humility;
and guide me to achievement.
I am incredibly successful.
I am constantly moving forward.

All success is born of failure. It is my stepping stone. I do not fear failure. I do not slow down if I have temporary setbacks; I can use what I have learned from the experience. I must capitalize on every setback I can learn from, so I do not have to endure the setback myself. Studying others' experiences moves me quicker to success in any aspect of life.

I am learning and
evolving each day.
My knowledge expands,
my abilities improve,
my capacity increases.
It is wonderful.
I can do anything
and the world is
at hand to assist me.
I am not a human being;
I am a human becoming.

It is an affront to the creator to suggest that he created a system that cannot excel.

There is never a time when I cannot learn, progress, and get better. The only exception is when I choose to say I cannot learn or change. Then, indeed, I cannot.

I own the world.
It is my planet.
I feel for its wounds.
I plead for its cities.
I see its poor and feeble.
I feel my need here.

When Christopher Columbus set foot in the New World and declared it for Spain, did he have the right? Not really. While the conqueror or "would be" conqueror may declare ownership, others may choose to defend their right to that possession or they may concede to not care what the new claimant thinks or says. Interestingly enough, most people do not care. In fact, you can literally lay claim to the city that you live in, the state that you reside in, a mountain, a star, and even the world! It is amazing how it will change your view of what your tenants are doing to your place. By changing your point of view, you will change the way you see things, others, and the world you own.

When I sleep at night
the wisdom of the ages enters
the playground of my mind.
I become one with greatness.
I soar in vision and
bathe in wisdom.
Slumber is my academy of
higher learning.
I strive to remember
what has transpired
and translate its meaning into
my everyday life.

We dream each night, yet often forget what has taken place. We discard the notion that we are important enough to receive visions and insights during our slumber. Are we not all called to the mission of protecting our planet? Do we all not have charge to build others and ourselves? Have we been forgotten by the universe or our God? Consider carefully what will transpire this next evening when your conscious mind is at rest, and your deep and predominant subconscious is in communion with life's higher powers.

I own my dream. It is mine.
I haven't yet taken
possession of it,
but it is mine.
It is written indelibly in
the corridors of my heart;
engraved deeply
into my mind;
it is a part of me.
My dream is etched
into my life and I own it.
I soon will take
possession of it,
and reap the rewards of
my patience and efforts.

When we layaway a gift for someone, it is theirs, even though they do not yet know it. It belongs to them, yet they are unaware. Even we do not have possession of it, but it is theirs. They have title, ownership, but not possession of their gift. So it is with us. If in our hearts there is a dream with a plan of action, then the dream belongs to us. We may not have it in our possession, but we own it. Reality is now only a matter of time.

I am fascinated by life.
I cannot get enough of it.
Everything I see
I want to know about.
There is so much to discover.
I must pick and
choose carefully,
where and how
I will spend my precious moments of living.

It was Thomas Carlyle who said, "The man who cannot wonder, habitually, wonder and wander, is but a pair of spectacles behind which there are no eyes." Remember when you were a child, how interesting a leaf was? The sun reflecting on a beetle's back. The loss of wonderment is the beginning of depression. The loss of appreciation for the nature of things and the beauty of our existence causes us to turn inward in a negative way — a self-destructive way.

I am wanted and needed
by tens of thousands of people.
I am admired
and they wish I was with them.

Somewhere, poor degraded people live in a village. If I could visit them they would welcome me as a leader. I would be wise, attractive, and wealthy. They would love me and want me to stay and lead them, teach them, and help them. There are millions of these people in this world waiting for me to touch their lives.

Life is full of fact and truth
I can count on.
My life is secure.
I make confident plans for
a better tomorrow.

For thousands of years, the sun has appeared on the eastern horizon. It has for the 6,000 years of man's recorded history, and it will again tomorrow.

I am a designer
of a quality life.
I orchestrate and direct
my own destiny.

We are all born with a designer's gene. It is the decisions we make that determine our future.

I am humble before God
and the universe.

I cannot create any living thing on earth. I cannot even make a grain of rice or a peppercorn. I have neither the knowledge nor the capability of creating life, even in procreation. I can only begin the process.

I am an artist;
An artist of sound,
sight and word.

I do not know what music is, or what it looks like. I need not know what is in modeling clay to make a vase. The ingredients of paint do not help me to paint. I do not know why rubbing metal makes it change color. Beauty is my opinion.

I have no defect that will keep
me from achieving greatness.
Greatness is mine.

Napoleon was short; Caesar stuttered; Beethoven was deaf; Helen Keller & John Milton were blind; Leonardo Da Vinci rarely finished his work; Benjamin Franklin flunked math; Albert Einstein and Winston Churchill failed their entrance test for school; Galileo was poor; Reggie Jackson struck out 2,597 times; and George Washington lost his first battles!

I love life.
I embrace each moment.
I love adventures.
I heal all wounds with others.
I improve with age.
I get younger each day.
I take good care of
my priceless body.

We will spend about 80 years on this planet.
How many more summers?
How many more springs?

My life is completely full of beauty and beautiful people.
I live in a beautiful world.

There is no logic in a God creating ugliness. It would never happen. Man is responsible for the term and its meaning.

I am at peace; I am calm;
and my soul is at rest.
I use all elements for
my progression,
and for
the progression of others.

Inside an airplane, I sit and look out the window. I see the great engine only inches away. The turbo fans spin at an incredible speed. With a flow of noxious fuel, the flames explode in a controlled burn, causing a deafening roar that I cannot hear from the comfort of my seat. Thousands of pounds of thrust through freezing cold air propel me in comfort and serenity.

**Money is abundant.
All that I could want or need
is all around me.
I can have anything I choose.**

Look around. How much did the building across the street cost? How much money was spent to build the road you drive on? The bank is full of money owned by people who have so much they want to lend their abundance to others. All that is needed to obtain money is a plan.

Copy these and make up your own. Make sure you do not "wish" for anything. An affirmation must be in the present tense, and be a statement of your life as though you have already attained your goal.

The best thing we can do this moment, for others, is work on ourselves. I believe after you have applied these affirmations the first time, other people are going to notice something about you that is different, something they like. Each time you repeat the affirmations, you and others will notice a difference.

◿ Important Note ◄

If you have read up to this point and do not intend to actually do what is being suggested, then you are wasting your energy. You are ingesting what Jim Rohn calls "mind candy." It is tasty, but in a day or so it will be forgotten, and you will be no better off than the Zirconia leader. I will have entertained you, but not helped you. I would like to challenge you to tear out or write down the pages that contain the affirmations and begin reading those until you have memorized them. Do this alone, and success as a leader will begin.

The *THIRD* thing we must do to reverse the eighty thousand negative inputs (plus all those received since we were ten years old) is *stop hanging around negative people!* Here is a polite thing you can say to them, *"You're Right. So What? GO AWAY!"*

Share your new attitude. It will really bug your negative friends. Tell them to get with it or get out! It will amaze you how your new found views will catch on positively with most everyone you associate with. For those who don't get it, move on. They will not follow.

These words may seem harsh, but believe me, those who would hold you back are not the friends you think they are. Success and wealth will take you to new places, and introduce you to new friends that will be forever dear and every bit as beloved as those you now associate with. The positive people will support and respect you, the negative people will be forgotten.

A leader has more than 100,000 admiring friends. Your organization is your new world and you will love it.

We must also halt any negativity in any form. Fight against it. Cancel the morning paper. Turn off the news. Ignore the gossips and complainers of the world, not forever, but exclusively for now. Chase away all negative people in your life. Turn them off! Declare with boldness, you will have no more of it.

I remember several years ago telling a sales companion about an individual in our organization named Lewis. I did not like him, and had lots of reasons I thought were quite valid. For two or three days, I went on espousing the bad qualities I felt Lewis had. On the third day, I said again, after a merciless assault, "I really can't stand that guy!" To my surprise, the person I was talking to said, "Me neither!" I said, "Wow! You mean all this time I have been talking about Lewis, you knew him?" He said "No, but I've heard so much about him from you, I can't stand him either!" I was exemplifying Zirconia leadership. I learned a great lesson that day.

Negative assaults on others, whether you are talking or listening, are like mud fights. All participants and all spectators get muddied.

Six weeks after this learning experience, I was at a training seminar with two hundred participants attending, including Lewis. I publicly apologized and asked that he forgive my ignorance. He did.

A leader remembers that we all wear a sign around our neck. It is totally invisible to the Zirconia, but it blinks in neon to the true leader. It says, *"Here I am. Make me important! Make me feel good about myself! Don't rain on my picnic! Don't snow on my parade! Don't blow out my candle! Don't stuff a quarter in my ear, and put your finger in my eye and try to dial a number! I AM SOMEBODY! MAKE ME IMPORTANT!"*

As a leader who is avoiding the negative folks and seeking out good folks, look for these hidden signs. Associate only with positive/motivated people, and the mind will react. Your life will change from black and white to living color. Negativity will flee; money will begin to check you out or as I have heard it said, "Dollars will come and dance in your backyard just to see what you are up to." Let's look at the possible logistics for a moment.

If you need eighty-one thousand positive affirmations to turn it all around in your life, then it requires you to hear, speak, or read one positive thing every six minutes for a year! Sounds impossible right? It's not. It is quite simple to do, and we are going to get started right now! Here are some examples:

Q: **"How's it going?"**

Zirconia:
"Okay, I guess..."

Diamond/Leader:
"*Incredible*, thanks for asking, *it's going really great!*"

Q: **"Are you going to the conference next week?"**

Zirconia:
"I don't know, I haven't made up my mind..."

Diamond/Leader:
"Wouldn't miss it! *I am having so much fun,* I find it hard to get it all in."

Q: **"Is it true you missed your plane last week?"**

Zirconia:
"Don't remind me. It's a bad memory."

Diamond/Leader:
"Yes, in Vancouver. I did some fantastic reading in a great little foodcourt."

Q: **"But weren't you upset about getting back late?"**

Zirconia:
"I am sick of that airline, they make cement look smart."

Diamond/Leader:
"Not really. If the plane, the pilot, or the weather is not going to perform perfectly, I would rather be on the ground reading a good book!"

In this short twenty-second example, we gave five positive responses. It is not easy at first, and it takes a great effort, but the results are sublime. Don't forget, you will not just change you. You will change everyone around you as you begin this transformation. Just think of it, a new you! Envision it. A new, energetic, positive being, that is happy in life, not miserable. It is there, inside you, waiting to emerge and consume you. Let out the new positive leader now. Get started today. Leaders need no reason to perform. They just DO IT!

Psychological Principle #11

LEADERS OF PEOPLE ARE POSITIVE AND EXCITED. IT IS THEIR NATURE!

It is not an act. Real leaders of people are positive, motivated, exciting people to be around. Zirconias seek admiration through self-promotion. True leaders do not seek admiration, but receive it through *attraction,* not *promotion.* So, perhaps you are asking how it is that people like Beethoven, Van Gogh or other historic people, whom we know were frequently sad or depressed, achieved leadership titles? Remember I said "leaders of people."

There is no question that some people can "lead" in artistic and other fields, but to lead people, one must carry a special responsibility. In the "art" of leading humans into achieving happiness or wealth, one cannot express the creativity that musicians or artists can enjoy. In art or music, the artist is free to express his feelings without concern for others' opinions. Unless offering a commercial service, the artist creates for his own fulfillment, without serious concern as to whether or not observers will enjoy, or even understand his work. But the "leader of people" must consider the fragility of others who have come to him with their unfulfilled dreams and cares. When one places trust in the leader of people, it borders the realm of sacred issues, and he cannot lead them astray.

Leaders must be more refined and careful not to make mistakes with other people's time and feelings. Leadership in a form which says, "Look at me. Follow me." is the highest form of leadership on our planet. No form is more noble, or grand in its scope and responsibility. Many people associate this human endeavor as almost divine in nature. It requires a mixture of humility, and yet boldness, temperance flavored with firm resolve and powerful decisiveness. True leaders of people take years to develop themselves, and must practice carefully on others during the process. For two thousand years, most of the inhabitants of this planet have isolated a man named Jesus to be the all time greatest leader of people. He is the only philosopher and teacher who actually said, "Come! Follow me." and "I am the way." His mission has so influenced humanity that our world has established his life as the Meridian of Time for all mankind. What a powerful sense of resolve and profound confidence. What vision! As best as I can tell, he only lived around thirty-three years, and it appears he took at least thirty years in preparation to make such declarations. Our missions do not relate to the lofty elevations of the eternal future of humanity. We are about helping folks enjoy their short experience on the revolving orb we call earth. Still, a leader must have courage and conviction to stand and say, "I have something that can help, I know something. Take my hand and I will lead you." Without a positive outlook on life, without confidence that your system or ideas will work, one cannot lead. At best, we can only give a good speech, dripping with delightful mind candy, and void of positive results.

IF and CAN'T — Two powerful words to contemplate.

Leaders are positive, not just in their talk, but in their nature. If they did not learn it in their youth, they *express-learn* it as an adult. Leaders totally believe in their cause. They do not care who gets credit for something they do. They spend significant amounts of time learning, teaching, and practicing leadership principles.

So do we BEGIN at age forty, fifty, or sixty if we don't know how? Do we have time? The answer is a resounding YES! YES! YES! Today, we can do ten-times-as-much and do it ten-times-faster than a decade ago. Information is abundant on how to quickly transform ourselves upward. My father could not just plug in a tape or find it on the Internet. Today the world is at our fingertips. Seminars are everywhere. Self-hypnosis, inner-child work, TV specials and libraries are everywhere in our lives. Our parents had a half-dozen good books and one record album with information on how to transform oneself into a successful leader. Today, you can spend ten dollars to join a Network Marketing company selling anything from vitamins to telephone cards, and be offered tens of thousands of dollars worth of personal development material. It is incredible. Equally amazing, however, is how many people do not take advantage of any of this. Russell Conwells famous story called "Acres of Diamonds" (about a man who searches the world for a fortune until he dies - a fortune he could have discovered in his own backyard) demonstrates the longevity of this disease I call the "scourge of complacency." Few things are as pathetic as untapped talent due to compromise.

In the dramatic film, "Papillon," a French criminal named Henri "The Butterfly," (Papillon in French) Charriere is sent to the Devil's Island penal colony. He declares he is innocent, and that he was framed. In a dream, he defends his position before an inquisition. There they inform him that they are punishing him for living a worthless life, not the crime for which he was convicted. He then realizes that he is "Guilty as charged."

We must have no regrets for our lives to this point, but must use our past to motivate ourselves to move forward. *The second we decide to be a leader and dedicate ourselves to great service, we pardon all our past.* Remember the past is only to inspire and teach others. Call back to memory those nuggets of wisdom that can uplift others. The past is a canceled check. The future is an unopened mine full of jewels and precious metals.

Cavett Robert, the great orator and principal founder of the National Speakers Association, told me a story about a little girl placing her tenth spoonful of sugar in a cup of herb tea. Her father asked, "Sweetheart, don't you think the tea will be too sweet?" "No daddy. Not if I don't stir it!" So it is with us. Thousands of stories deep within that make us what we are, go untapped. The wisdom that could lift our world is left in the shadows of our memory. Leaders tell their stories, and share the wisdom they have accumulated. It is never too late to begin. As Zig Ziglar once said, *"We are going to live a lot longer off this planet than we are on it."* No matter what our age is, now is the time to lead. Now is the moment to begin.

✐ Important Note ✎

We often do not remember the things that make us who we are, but they did, in reality, happen, and now we live with the results, whether they are positive or negative in nature.

I had a sixth grade teacher that drove me crazy. His name was Mr. Tipton. I didn't like him because he was a good teacher. There is an unwritten law that says if food or people are good for you when you are in the sixth grade, you cannot like them. I remember only three things about Mr. Tipton. He made us memorize two poems, which at the time seemed to me like epic poems.

We had to deliver the poems in front of the class in order to graduate. I apparently made it because I got a diploma, but I do not remember my performance. We forget the event at the time, but its effect always manifests itself later in our life.

The poems were "IF" by Rudyard Kipling, and "CAN'T" by Edgar Guest. As you read these poems, (that I had to learn against my desires) imagine the good they have subconsciously done for me over the years.

"If"

If you can keep your head when all about you
  Are losing theirs and blaming it on you;
If you can trust yourself when all men doubt you,
  But make allowance for their doubting too;
If you can wait and not be tired by waiting,
  Or, being lied about, don't deal in lies,
  Or being hated don't give way to hating,
  And yet don't look too good, nor talk too wise;

If you can dream-and not make dreams your master;
If you can think-and not make thoughts your aim,
If you can meet with Triumph and Disaster
  And treat those two imposters just the same:
If you can bear to hear the truth you've spoken,
  Twisted by knaves to make a trap for fools,
  Or watch the things you gave your life to, broken,
  And stoop to build 'em up with worn out tools;

If you can make one heap of all your winnings
  And risk it on one turn of pitch-and-toss,
  And lose, and start again at your beginnings,
  And never breathe a word about your loss;
If you can force your heart and nerve and sinew,
  To serve your turn long after they are gone,
  And so hold on when there is nothing in you,
  Except the Will which says to them: "Hold on!"

If you can talk with crowds and keep your virtue,
  Or walk with Kings - nor lose the common touch,
If neither foes nor loving friends can hurt you,
If all men count with you, but none too much:
  Yours is the Earth and everything that's in it,
  And - which is more –
  You'll be a man my son!

~ Rudyard Kipling

"Can't"

Can't is the worst word that's written or spoken
  Doing more harm here than slander and lies;
  On it is many a strong spirit broken,
  And with it many a good purpose dies.
  It springs from the lips of the thoughtless each morning
  And robs us of courage we need through the day
  It rings in our ears like a timely sent warning
  And laughs when we falter and fall by the way.

Can't is the father of feeble endeavor,
  The parent of terror and halfhearted work;
  It weakens the efforts of artisans clever,
  And makes of the toiler an indolent shirk.
  It poisons the soul of the man with a vision,
  It stifles in infancy many a plan;
  It greets honest toiling with open derision,
  And mocks at the hopes and dreams of a man.

Can't is a word none should speak without blushing;
  To utter it should be a symbol of shame;
  Ambition and courage it daily is crushing;
  It blights a man's purpose and shortens his aim.
  Despise it with all your hatred of error;
  Refuse it the lodgment it seeks in your brain;
  Arm against it as a creature of terror;
  And all that you dream of you someday shall gain.

Can't is the word that is foe to ambition,
  An enemy ambush to shatter your will;
  Its prey is forever the man with a mission,
  And bows but to courage and patience and skill.
  Hate it, with hatred that's deep and undying,
  For once it is welcomed 'twill break any man;
  Whatever the goal you are seeking, keep trying,
  And answer this demon by saying: "I can."

~ Edgar A. Guest

Read these poems on a daily basis; memorize them if you like. They will transform your attitude upward at a jet-like speed.

Beware of the Zirconia tendency to read it once or twice, and never attempt to internalize the wisdom offered.

There are two stanzas of another poem by Henry Wadsworth Longfellow that describe being pro-active by nature.

"Something Left Undone"

Labor with what zeal you will,
Something still remains undone,
Something uncompleted still,
Waits the rising of the sun.

Till at length the burden seems,
Greater than the strength can bear;
Heavy as the weight of dreams
Pressing on us everywhere.

~ Henry Wadsworth Longfellow

While most of us enjoy our dreams, to those who procrastinate using their talents, dreams are a torment, weighing on them like a curse, like the desert wanderer always taunted by the mirage of water, just out of reach, and not really there.

Leaders ACT on what they have learned. They act mentally, physically, emotionally, and spiritually.

3 x 5 CARD

> *My mind is a library of wisdom and wit.*
> *I am always adding to its shelves.*
> *(Memorize a poem, write it down, and*
> *practice it until you have learned it)*

Yes, I remember all of us youth vilifying Mr. Tipton. We thought to ourselves, "What kind of evil teacher would force happy-go-lucky kids like us to learn such poetry that we did not even understand?" I am so glad he was such a tyrant. He did wonders for me, and now perhaps you too!

I said he did three things that I remember, however, two things were memorizing the two poems. The other experience I can never forget was that he cried. He cried when they assassinated President John F. Kennedy. We did not understand at the time why he did that, but we never forgot it. It was the only time we ever saw him "down" or sad. He was always "up" except for that day.

Leaders are not only teachable and pro-active, GREAT leaders are vulnerable as was Mr. Tipton. There will always be events that will try us and push us to the limit. It is at the edge of the abyss that the medals, pins, and honors great leaders receive are truly earned. Generally, the day after a tragic event, the leader is again "up." Leaders carry on, and on, and on!

The Zirconia plays a different game. Earlier, I mentioned that no matter what, "You're right!" Well, the Zirconia will play a tragedy for all it is worth, using it as a crutch, or reason why success has eluded him. The cure for this, is to get back on the horse immediately after you have fallen. Don't wait.

I remember, in high school, I was terrified of the trampoline. I don't know why, but to me it was not fun. I was instructed in P.E. class to do a three-quarter back flip, landing on my stomach. I hesitated, but went for it at the relentless urging of my classmates and the coach. "OOF!" I landed on the edge, stomach on the frame, and then slid off to the ground on my back. I lay for a moment, opened my eyes, and saw everyone standing around me staring. "Are you dead?" Were the first words I heard. My coach said to get right back up and try it again. Now mind you, I hated the thing in the first place, and had no initial desire to inflict such pain on myself once, let alone twice. This idiot wanted me to do it again. Reluctantly, I was forced to get back up and try it again. To make this story really work, I could tell you about my triumphant second try, and how I landed on my stomach perfectly in the middle of the trampoline, and how my idiot (brilliant) coach and I were the heroes of the day, right? It didn't happen like that. I got up, did it again, and landed on the edge again. "OOF!" (Now he was a double idiot.) That was it, over with, done, finis! I had learned two important things that day and my coach was happy. First, trampolines and I would never be friends, and second, GET UP AGAIN! No matter what, get up and at it again. Years would pass before I would realize what my coach had done for me. The true leader will always be "up," at least whenever he is seen by others. His *job* is to be "up." It is his responsibility and a major purpose he is fulfilling. So, if you are not already the "up" leader, how is it possible that, as a leader-in-training, you can always be "up?" Should you fake it? It is not "faking" if you have made a positive mental and heartfelt decision to change.

Harland Stonecipher learned about being "up" at a young age. And when tragedy struck in July 1969, in a near fatal auto accident, his ability to see possibility in adversity paid off in a big way. After being hospitalized for several days, he discovered the driver that caused the accident *might sue him!* During his recovery, Harland realized the need for legal insurance in America. He decided to create something that had never before been done in the U.S. Out of the ashes of disaster, without money or much experience they began. "We better think big, or not think at all," was his attitude. And think big he did. Recently, his company hit a market cap value in excess of one billion dollars on the American Stock Exchange. This type of success in the WBI means many personal success stories are being made every day and Stonecipher says, "...the best is yet to come!"

There are some secrets to always staying "up" and I will share them with you.

Psychological Principle #12
LEADERS GET UP
TIME AND TIME AGAIN
UNTIL...

For example, true leaders accept that they have a responsibility to be examples. They accept that they are worthy of more than they have, and they accept that anyone who is committed can achieve his dreams. What is that secret something that leaders have that sets them apart from others, that ability to always be cheery and up? It is a power they possess, and most leaders have forgotten they have it.

Leaders often will not even realize the most valuable asset they have is a power, a hidden force they use every single day.

How can they use it, and not know they have it?

There is a story that explains how habits rob us of appreciation. The greatest library the world has ever known was the Library of Alexandria. Founded when the city was built by Alexander the Great in 332 BC, this incredible library is reputed to have been the greatest ever created. It contained more than one-half million books (scrolls) and was the center of information for the entire world then. It stood for seven- hundred years, and then was burned by the Christians in 391 A.D. After the burning, a legend was born that one book survived. A poor man found the book, and studied to learn how to read the writings. The book told of how one could transform metal into gold, but only with the aid of a rare "touchstone." To find the touchstone, one had to go to the beaches of a sea called Pontus Axeinus (Black Sea), three hundred leagues to the north. There, one had to pick up the stones on the shores and hold them to the cheek. If a warm stone was found, it would be the "Touchstone." The man gave up all he had, and traveled a thousand miles, and for three years looked for the stone. Each day he would spend hours touching cold stones to his face. One day he picked up a stone, touched it to his cheek, and then threw it into the sea. He then realized it was the warm stone. He had thrown his fortune away because of habit. He had gained a habit of throwing stones into the sea, and when the one stone he was searching for came along, he threw it away.

We all do the same thing every day. In our younger years we learned things that we now take for granted, and when we need the answer, or "touchstone," we throw the wisdom away. Remember, "A penny saved is a penny earned?" No, we did not save our pennies. We wish we had, but we did not. So what is the secret thing we knew that we have forgotten? Is it that leaders do not take what they know for granted? Perhaps that is true, but there is no special power here. Is it that Leaders have forgotten how to care more about others, than themselves? Well, that is a leadership principle also, but it is not the big one.

Leaders subconsciously use a special power, what is it? It is a power that makes their life and the lives of others complete! It is a power that takes away the anger in life and brings one the things he wants, a power that puts a jump in the step, a smile on the face when no one is looking, a power that frees the mind and spirit from unseen bondage.

Leaders use the most powerful secret known to humans, inadvertently, having forgotten when they realized it.

Leaders subconsciously acknowledge they have the power of CHOICE!

Years ago, someone told us, "You can do anything." When we were young and impressionable, we heard this and believed it. Now, it seems we have forgotten it, and we don't know why we lead, we just lead. We just accept possibility thinking. We forget why.

Leaders just *choose* to have great days. Leaders just *choose* to succeed and to work when they don't have to. Leaders just *choose* not to stop because they are tired. Leaders just *choose* to be happy, smart, successful, clever, sharp, and sometimes, COOL.

They do not need someone's permission to have it all, to be a success. They just *choose* to go for it. Someone else's label on them means nothing to them. Their own label is all that matters.

Psychological Principle #13
LEADERS UNDERSTAND THE POWER OF CHOICE

Ninety-eight percent of all WBI distributors, ninety-eight percent of all the people using the MLM/Network Marketing sales technique, ninety-eight percent of all the entrepreneurs on the planet DO NOT UNDERSTAND THIS ONE MONUMENTAL POINT.

It is so fundamental, so simple, and so unbelievably basic, that NINETY-EIGHT OUT OF 100 WILL MISS IT!

We have the power to choose success! We can choose to win! We can choose, right now, to be on top, to be happy, to associate with winners, to be rich! We have the power of choice.

If progression has ceased in your business, you have the power to start it up again. Dan McCormick says, "This is where you find out if you truly love the journey, or the process, or working with people, or if you are just in it for the money. The true leader loves the journey; it's why I keep doing it everyday, even when I don't have to after 17 years." *You can throw the switch.* It is all up to you. It is like a power generator, which provides electricity. It is inside your head. You have the whole thing, lying dormant, waiting for you to turn it on. Your friends cannot do it for you. Your family cannot help you. It is all up to you. Conditions do not have to be right, and the weather does not matter, you simply must throw the switch.

If you have been grumpy, you have the power to choose a different way of greeting people. You have the power of controlling conversations. You can walk away from a conversation that is not going the way you want it to. You can change environments. If you have had a tendency to be reclusive, you can become more accessible to people. You can choose to change your dress code, your face (to smile more) and even the handshake you offer people. It is all up to you!

3 x 5 CARD

> *I am free to choose.*
> *I am in control of*
> *the most powerful force in the universe,*
> CHOICE.
> *(Ponder on this statement for 15 minutes)*

You can *choose* to be rich, by using the numbers game and the MLM sales technique to acquire money. It is academic. You can choose to go through the numbers whenever you wish to! One-out-of-ten is going to say, "Yes," to look at whatever you choose to present or say, "Yes," to a purchase. You can *choose* to ask twenty people a day to buy or look at something with the expectation that most will say "No." You can choose today to begin the journey to success, ...if you want to!

✍ Important Note ✎

Out of 100 that are reading this page, only two are making the decision to talk to twenty people per day until they get the money they want. Another two are already doing it. Where do you stand? Sometimes it is wonderful to awaken the giant within us, and sometimes it is painful to face the realities of our own desire to lead. It is our choice either way. And remember, any reason why you will not do what is necessary, is valid. "Twenty is too many." "You're right!" "I don't have time." "You're right!" "Drew Earl doesn't know what he is talking about." "You're right!" "I don't believe it." "You're right!" "I am a leader now. I need to manage my organization." "You're right!" "You only need to talk to three a day." "You're right!" But the bottom line is, it is your choice, and numbers never lie.

Twenty people-a-day would be a tough choice to make. But leaders are people who make tough choices, and stick with them. As Jim Rohn says, "How long?" "UNTIL!" "Until when?" "UNTIL!" Many people want the easy choices — the soft choices, and that is okay; there is just no money in easy choices. It is a *tough* choice to work for riches. It is an *easy* choice to work hard. Digging a ditch is hard work, but an easy choice. Talking to strangers is easy work, but a tough choice. One will make you rich! One will keep you poor. It is a tough choice, but you have the *power to choose* either one. Which one do you want badly enough?

You have been who you are for many years. Do you want to change? Tough choice. Leaders make tough choices. Are you ready to become something better than you are? Are you ready to stretch?

One young man, in the year 1733, made the decision to better himself through a "bold and arduous project of arriving at moral perfection." In his zeal, he soon discovered *"perfection"* is not all that easy. He writes, "But I soon found I had undertaken a task of more difficulty than I had imagined, while my attention was taken up in guarding against one fault, I was often surprised by another." Nevertheless, this young man was determined and had made a CHOICE and commitment to improve himself, so he drafted twelve "virtues" that he dedicated himself to pursue. He later spoke with a religious friend who added one more, which made it the Thirteen Virtues of Benjamin Franklin. They are as follows:

1. **Temperance.**
   Eat not to dullness, and drink not to elevation.

2. **Silence.**
   Speak not but what may benefit others or yourself.
   Avoid trifling conversation.

3. **Order.**
   Let all your things have their places;
   let each part of your business have its time.

4. **Resolution.**
   Resolve to perform what you ought;
   perform without fail what you resolve.

5. **Frugality.**
   Make no expense but to do good to others or yourself;
   that is, waste nothing.

6. **Industry.**
Lose no time; be always employed in something useful;
cut off all unnecessary actions.

7. **Sincerity.**
Use no hurtful deceit; think innocently and justly; and,
if you speak, speak accordingly.

8. **Justice.**
Wrong none by doing injuries, or
omitting the benefits that are your duty.

9. **Moderation.**
Avoid extremes; forbear resenting injuries,
so much as you think they deserve.

10. **Cleanliness.**
Tolerate no uncleanliness in body, clothes or habitation.

11. **Tranquillity.**
Be not disturbed at trifles, or at accidents common or
unavoidable.

12. **Chastity.**
Rarely use venery but for health or offspring;
never to dullness, weakness, or the injury of your own or
another's peace or reputation.

13. **Humility.**
Imitate Jesus and Socrates.

from "Autobiography of Benjamin Franklin."

What a successful life this great man lived. He chose to succeed. He could have chosen to be just another life that came and went during the 1700's. But he made "CHOICES." He made the right choices.

While we appreciate the noble "virtues" that Ben left us, let us apply thirteen of our own that can address the challenges to building a successful business.

1. ***Today I choose to be rich!***
   I will apply the Law of Cause and Effect,
   to achieve wealth over the next five years.

2. ***Today I choose to do whatever it takes!***
   I will listen to those who have done it,
   and follow them until my earnings exceed theirs.

3. ***Today I choose to enter the FEAR zone.***
   I will abandon the COMFORT zone of my life.
   When I think I need a COMFORT zone,
   I will find the ADVENTURE zone.

4. ***Today I choose to invite.***
   My new life is made up of inviting people
   to places they have never been,
   and heights they have never experienced.

5. ***Today I choose to learn.***
   I am back in school!
   I will stay there until I know everything!

6. *Today I choose to be a mentor.*
    Someone needs me. I will find them, and be there for them.

7. *Today I choose to believe.*
    I believe in the possibility
    and the extreme probability of my success.

8. *Today I choose to DESERVE.*
    I deserve success. I will have it. I will not be denied!

9. *Today I choose to LOVE hearing "NO!"*
    A "no" means a "yes" is on the way.
    Give me eighteen-a-day, and I will sponsor two!

10. *Today I choose to totally control my mind,*
    my emotions, and my actions.
    How dare someone try to steal my dream!
    It cannot happen. It is my choice.

11. *Today I choose to enjoy life.*
    I travel; I sleep on beaches, climb mountains,
    and inhale life. Joy no longer hides from me.
    It is all around me.

12. *Today I choose to care.*
    So many want a better life. I can help them!

13. *Today I choose to LEAD!*
    It is about time I got off my "buts."
    I have no excuse for action except for positive results.
    I AM A LEADER!

How many can you think of? Develop *your* own choices. Determine what success is to *you*. You say how far, how high, and how long you want to go.

Gaining a deep understanding of the universal nature and power of choice is essential for one to be able to stand with the courage of their convictions, and not move downward under pressure from foes or peers. These timely words were penned over a hundred years ago by William C. Gregg; they put into perspective the tremendous power of choice:

> *" Know this, that every soul is free,*
> *To choose his life and what he'll be;*
> *For this eternal truth is given,*
> *That God will force no man to heaven.*
>
> *He'll call, persuade, direct aright,*
> *And bless with wisdom, love, and light;*
> *In nameless ways be good and kind,*
> *But never force the human mind."*

~ *William C. Gregg circa 1840*

Never underestimate the incredible power of choice. It is a power of which you are in complete control, and when understood, will rapidly change your world for the better. A man asked me the other day, "How do you know when you are successful?" I said that it depends on what you conceive success to be. The mountain man will not be happy in a pinstriped suit, living near Wall Street. Likewise, the banker will probably not be happy on a mule in the snow. Success is like beauty. It resides in the beholder.

And what of the Zirconias? They are the sad souls who can never make a decision on what they want. They flit-

and-flitter from one "happy hope" to another. They cannot stand by their choices when they do make them. They wander like the *"trash flies"* from one "Oh boy!" to another, never applying the disciplines necessary to have their dreams come true. They reside in the city of Compromise and Contentment. They seek the easiest possible plan, which promises everything for nearly nothing. They do not know "hot" or "cold." My father used to call such non-decision makers, *"mugwump birds."* He described them as big, ugly birds that sat on fences with their "mug" on one side, and their "wump" on the other.

President Theodore Roosevelt said, *"Far better it is to dare mighty things, to win glorious triumphs even though check-ered by failure, than to rank with those poor spirits who neither enjoy nor suffer much because they live in the gray twilight that knows neither victory nor defeat."* Such miserable folks make one-sided choices, risking no loss, blind-siding themselves to the fact that such decisions forever keep them from winning. They make a choice to be safe, warm, and mediocre. No leadership is needed there. Even John, the writer of a book that we know as "Revelation" in the Bible implies that there is no place for the indolent in the eyes of deity. Quoting Jesus, John writes, *"I would thou wert cold or hot. So then because thou art lukewarm, and neither cold nor hot, I will spue thee out of my mouth."* (Revelation 3:15,16 KJV)

If, indeed, John was speaking the very words of Jesus, then there is no place on earth, or in heaven for people who cannot make a choice.

So how can the Zirconia, who always vacillates, hope

to build a business that leads people into wealth and freedom, when he can't decide whether to make some three-way-calls, or watch TV? When a person cannot make a decision whether to buy a case of beer, or a case of saleable products, how can they succeed? The Zirconia will cause you to think he is 100 percent committed, but in reality he only does the business if it drops in his lap, and that he does only on meeting night. The Zirconia will never know the joy of Providence or Luck. Both of these great allies make all the necessary breaks for the committed leaders. We will talk more about both shortly.

It is necessary for me to mention here, that the day you decide to begin making hard, correct, choices is the beginning of your success, no matter what your age or your current financial situation is. Remember, Ray Kroc never graduated from high school and was fifty-two years old when he bought a hamburger enterprise from Mac and Rich McDonald in 1954. Before his death, he was a billionaire, and, an American Tradition.

3 x 5 CARD

> *I lead only where I have earned*
> *the right to lead.*
> *I accept myself as a leader, and I accept*
> *myself as a student and as an apprentice in*
> *areas where I am still earning*
> *the rights of leadership.*
> *(Ask "May I show you?" and*
> *"Will you show me?" today)*

Psychological Principle #14
LEADERS START
WITH A CLEAR VISION OF THE END!

Perhaps you are one who has tried and failed a few times. I know of one man who took pride in declaring that he had been in thirty-two different opportunities! He was proud of it! As my kids would say, "Go figure!" We have covered enough information for you to decide what kind of entrepreneur he was, and why he probably did not succeed in his business. The question is, can he succeed if he tries again? The answer is YES, but only if he determines that he wants to be more than just a starter. Finishing a personal goal is primary to the success of a WBI professional.

If you have failed so many times that you no longer want to try again, then I have some questions for you, "What did the picture of success look like when you were first starting out?" "Did you begin with the end in mind?" "Or did you just begin?" Many thousands of people begin something then *fail*, only to go on to *succeed*. The difference is they had a picture of success in their minds and they resolved to stick with it until they won.

I have personally seen the anguish of several MLM company leaders who did not know how they were going to keep the doors open one more day. The distributors never knew it! The owners anguished alone, but succeeded against all odds, because they knew what the eventual success was going to offer. They would let the world quit them, but they were not going to quit the world.

To the leader, failure is a temporary condition, a learning experience. To the leader, disappointment is a possibility, but discouragement is not. To the leader, success requires getting up after falling down, because the end is already determined. They SEE it.

Winston Churchill failed a few times. He failed at school. He nearly failed at Sandhurst Academy after making three attempts to get in. He failed to be in the cavalry, and had to settle for being in the infantry. He failed in his father's eyes, and in the eyes of other family members. When he graduated and was commissioned, he missed his first promotion. He got captured in South Africa in the Boer War. He resigned his military commission to enter politics, and lost his first election campaign. Eventually he won, narrowly, and for several years served turbulently in the British Parliament. In 1911, he was transferred to the Admiralty. He readied the Navy for war, but in a short time he had alienated himself, having made several bad decisions, including losing battles and soldiers. He was demoted by the Conservatives of Parliament. He resigned from government service altogether. He quit! He returned to military service as an officer, and in 1917 entered Parliamentary service again. In 1922 he lost the election and again was out! In 1923 he lost again. In 1924 he lost by 43 votes. Later in the same year he won an election, and served five years before he again resigned his post. By 1931, "He had arrived at a point, where for all his abilities he was distrusted by every party. He was thought to lack judgement and stability and was regarded as a guerrilla fighter impatient of discipline." We could go on with the down sides of this great leader's life, but it should be sufficient information to show that losing is part of winning, and that leaders keep joining battles, with a vision of the end of the battle in their mind.

The Zirconia will join with no vision of success in mind. He will talk a good story of what might be, but will rarely say, "I'll be there first." He will readily commit you to something, but rarely commit himself to anything.

Leaders understand the "Bank of Providence."

Did you ever notice how "lucky" leaders are? The fact is, luck is how a loser spells success. Understanding the *Bank of Providence*, or luck, and how to make withdrawals from it, is an important factor in obtaining time and money freedom. It is a rather technical issue, so we will walk through the details together.

First, it is necessary to determine your worth in the marketplace. I did not say your worth as a member of the human race, or as a child of the universe, but your worth in market value.

⚜ Important Note ⚜

Your value, as a human being, is incalculable. But just for thought, how much would you take for your eyes? A million dollars? How about a hand? A finger? A man in Florida recently ran an ad in the newspaper offering his kidney for a sailboat! Value? About $65,000 to $125,000. He is sixty-five years old and figures someone else might want one of his two good kidneys in exchange for his being able to sail for the rest of his life. Interesting! How much are you worth as a human? A fortune!

So, what we want to know is. "What is our worth in the marketplace?" For starters, let us realize that we are primarily valued by what it would take to replace us. Then there are some other factors, minor issues, such as how much we are liked, how long we have been working and how good we are at what we do. But the main point is how much would it cost to replace us! For example, a janitor for a hospital can be replaced for relatively few dollars. Even though he may have been a janitor for thirty-five years and have a doctorate in *"Floor Mopping and Related Principles."* He is not going to make much in that profession. It says nothing of his value in the community or in a spiritual sense. A janitor could be the head of a local church, or even a federal judge. None of this value helps in the hospital arena. Now the value of a brain surgeon is a different story. Even if he is fresh out of school and green as grass, if someone needs a brain surgeon, they are going to pay a significant amount of money for him. And even on the social and spiritual level, nothing will matter. He could be a social scoundrel; worship crickets; and bury dead animals in his back yard during a full moon. He is still going to get paid by the value it takes to replace his services. He will make more than the janitor will.

Now, here is why we want to determine our value in the marketplace. If you know more about what you are worth, and the value of your time, you will be easily motivated to take better advantage of your opportunities. You will be more aware of them, and what you can do with them.

The first thing you need to do is ascertain what it costs you to watch television. How much money did you pay for your television? Write that figure down. Let's assume it is $500, it could be any amount, but we will say $500. Next, calculate the most money you ever made in a consistent work effort over at least two weeks time. Let's say it was $1,500. Divide $1,500 by 80 hours of work time. That gives you $18.75 per hour. Next, add up how much time you watch television: the news, a game on Saturday, maybe a sitcom or two, and a documentary on Sunday. Let's say about 6 hours a week. Now multiply that by 52 weeks a year; it equals about 312 hours a year or $5,850/year. So if you watch television 312 hours per year, based on your market value, (the most you ever consistently made is your value to the marketplace, no matter what you are doing at this time) then your television that you paid five hundred dollars for is COSTING you $5,850! WOW!

If you want to be a leader, you must take a non-erasable felt pen, and write this figure on the upper right-hand corner of the TV screen. There, it reminds you of what you could be doing instead of watching the "boob-tube." If you feel you can afford to watch another show at that price, you have definitely arrived!

Zirconias will write the amount on the screen in a dry marker, so it will fade away shortly. They will be making some notes so they can teach this stuff to their organization later. (Warning! Their words will be hollow, but they will look good.)

Now that we understand our value in the marketplace and the cost of watching television, let us discuss providence and how it works. Then, we will tie this together.

There is a bank called the *Bank of Providence*. It works very similarly to a money bank, but it deals in good works and service. It is very real. If you choose to disbelieve in it, that's okay, but it does not go away, it is always there.

It functions much like a conventional bank, although it deals in what some people call luck and others call blessings. *When you offer good genuine service through honorable leadership, you make a deposit.* When you fail to perform to the best of your abilities, a payment is paid out. MOST PEOPLE KNOW NOTHING OF THIS BANK. Still, day in and day out, it correctly calculates your account. Silently, secretly, the balance ledger climbs, and falls. No one knows what each of our balance sheets reflects, but often, we can guess pretty close.

If your value is $18.75 per hour, who paid for your omission of work and service while you sat in front of a TV? I am not saying you should not watch any TV. I am pointing out that you are reading this book on leadership! You would not be reading it if you did not want to improve, right? Why are you reading? Do you want to succeed? Do you want more money? Do you want time and money freedom? Do you want to be respected, and appreciated as a leader? If so, then your desires need to be attended to, and any lazy time spent doing nothing, when you could be doing something, must be paid for. *Once you make a commitment, the universe has a strong sense of contractual understanding that requires both parties to follow through.* The world owes you nothing, and it will deny you nothing. The world will allow any price to be extracted from it, but it will demand equal service rendered for payment made. That payment is deducted from your own account. Providential blessings are earned over and above genuine service. Where no service is rendered, (watching TV) how can one expect luck to season his life? Perhaps the luck you want cannot be paid for right now, because the money was spent to watch a sitcom. The "void of opportunity" is a reflection of your falling prey to procrastination and lazy wasted time, when you could have done more.

Is this hard for you to think about? Is your CM (conscious mind) trying to argue with it, and justify your COMFORT zone? Don't worry, the COMFORT zone will be there if you are not ready to step into the FEAR zone yet.

I believe if you are reading this book, and you are this far into it, then you are already a leader. I believe you have an account! I believe you perhaps did not know about it, and now you can take advantage of it. I believe you are an honorable person, and have done an abundant amount of good and noble things that have been credited to your account. Now it's time to use some of it to excel!

So how can we tap into the luck or providence that we may have in our account? *Let us start with an understanding that life is ready to give you anything you want, if only you want it bad enough.*

LEADERS DEMAND HELP FROM POWERS GREATER THAN THEM

I bargained with Life for a penny,
And Life would pay no more,
However I begged at evening,
When I counted my scanty store;

For Life is just an employer,
He gives you what you ask,
But once you have set the wages,
Why, you must bear the task.

I worked for a menial's hire,
Only to learn, dismayed,
That any wage I had asked of Life,
Life would have paid.

~ Jessie B. Rittenhouse, 1918

When you enter a bank where you have an account, how do you withdraw your money? Is it your money, or the bank's money? Yours, of course, so to get it out, first you fill out a withdrawal form. It may be a check, or slip of paper filled out at the counter. Having submitted the proper identification, you are presented with money that is yours, just not in your possession. It is the same at the *Bank of Providence*. If you demand, having rightfully earned what is due you, the bank pays every time! On the other hand, when too much has been paid out, and you are in "overdraft protection" mode, you may be faced with the stark reality that some service is in order to replenish the account. Remember that the account may have been paying your rent for inactivity. I have heard it said, *"Service is the rent we pay to live on earth and breath air."*

The Wealth Building Industry provides an abundant opportunity to make providential deposits. Understanding the "NO" is the key. When you regularly present people with the opportunity to join and succeed in a Network Marketing business, you are winning, even in rejection. People do not reject us. They reject your offer, but you offer it anyway, and that is what is important! That is the key. Do you see? Do you realize that it is like a doctor offering free medical service to the poor? You are offering freedom from financial bondage. You are offering time freedom: time to spend with kids, to travel, or just to read. You are offering people a chance to be their own boss, to take control of their own destiny. You are offering a happier life to people. Many, if not most, generally are too close-minded, or just plain too dumb, to take you up on the offer, but that is their problem, not yours.

So even if you may not make immediate cash every time you pitch someone, you should know you are depositing in the *Bank of Providence* that which you can withdraw later. Do you see the nobility here? It does not matter whether you are offering car polish, or baby soap if what you are offering is attached to an opportunity for a more fulfilling life.

I once emptied my account and went into overdraft mode. It was a tough time in my life. It was following a period of moderate success our family had experienced from 1984 to about 1988. During this time, I forgot about service to others, and was quite caught up in my own world. "What's in it for me?" was the line of the day. Then life took the proverbial "turn" that we all need from time to time to keep things in perspective.

In a ten-day span of time, I learned some great lessons about life and luck. The first thing I learned is that tragedy, luck, or bad weather is no respecter of people. They take their turn on you at will and there is not much you can do about it but act, or react. In ten days, the weather turned bad, we lost our income, our dish-washer broke, our washing machine broke, our dryer broke, our van quit running, and our electric box blew up on the back of our home! Some compassionate service groups deposited into the *Bank of Providence* by donating some food to our family, and paying our rent. Having no electricity in the house, I strung an electric cord to my neighbor's house (remember Al?), and asked if I could borrow some of his. He said it was okay. The refrigerator then promptly broke down, and the charity food spoiled. My wife bundled up the kids, (all five) and kissed me on the forehead, and went to stay at her sister's home for a while. I was to get our home back together again. I struggled for a few days in total anger at what "life was doing to me." Oh poor me! What did I do? Our house was dark and dismal. I knew without money it was going to take weeks, maybe months, maybe even years, to get our life back to normal. With no electrical power, the doors were open all the time, and the mud from the rain was tracked in a path from the front door to the back. I felt like a major failure.

One evening as I was trying to figure out what disaster I should work on next, my phone rang. It still worked! It was my son's scout group. I had volunteered to help on the Planning Committee. They wanted me to come to a meeting at a local restaurant and help plan a six-month calendar for the boys. I was not happy about this. I was definitely not in the mood for a bunch of rowdy, red-knee-socked backpackers from Troop 375. Surely, they would understand my dilemma. Surely, they would forgive and excuse me under all my weighty problems. I had a perfect and legitimate reason to "zirc-out big time!" If ever a Zirconia excuse would work, now was the time to spring it on them. But something in me said, *"You promised to serve."* Nevertheless, they were *just* Boy Scouts! Come on! Look at my miserable life, and all my justified reasons to stay home in my misery! Again, I felt the tug of leadership, *"You made a commitment!"*

So, I walked to my motorcycle (the only transportation I had left). I noticed my hands were greasy from working on my van. My blue jeans were dirty. I smelled like a mechanic after three days of hard work in the Arabian Desert, in August...with no shade! I did not care how I looked, so I put on my helmet and headed out to the meeting. I had one consolation, and in retrospect, it was probably the strongest reason I was going. FREE FOOD! As I approached an intersection, and came to a stop, I heard a loud "pop" on my helmet. Rain. RAIN. *RAIN!* I couldn't believe it. After all this, now God was going to rain on me while I was on my stupid motorcycle. I bottomed out at that moment. I gave up. In a daze of hopelessness, I drove on. I sat at the table dripping wet. The local scouts' advisor and church leader, Bob Walker, sat next to me. "How ya doin' bud?" he asked. I answered, "Fine." He looked at me deeply and asked, as only a spiritual leader can, "Why don't I believe you?" I knew I was had, so I laughingly responded that I was okay, but my washer, dryer, van, dishwasher, refrigerator and electric box had all died. I was broke, and embarrassed that my wife and kids had gone (until I could get our family's needs under control) — not to mention that I was soaked from riding my motorcycle in the rain. He smiled with me and went on with the meeting. As I struggled to be civil and somewhat effective helping the boys plan some camp-outs and service projects, I failed to notice that Bob left the table for a short while. (It seems he made some phone calls.) We finished the meeting, and I headed into the rain to go home.

When I drove up my street, I saw a man with a two-wheeled "dolly" taking a new refrigerator into my front door. Another man was under my van working on it. Another man was coming out of my backyard with a blown-up fuse box in his hand. To sum it up, my life turned around that very afternoon. It would not take months to get it together; it would only take a day.

As time has passed, I have reflected on that day, *"the day my life turned around."* What was it that happened? It was the fulfillment of a commitment, nothing more. I had used up all my luck. It was time for me to learn something and to pass a test. If I had not gone to that scout meeting —if I had chosen to stay home in my justified misery, I would not have been interviewed by Bob Walker. Both he and I fulfilled our commitments to young men who do not yet understand what they did that day. So we met each other at the right time and place. For a change, I made the right choice, and what would have taken months to fix under my own selfish pride, took one day. Providence followed commitment. Many people were at my home, serving, depositing into *their* accounts at the *Bank of Providence* for later need. It was time for me to humbly learn to receive and be grateful.

My whole outlook on life changed that day. Sometimes, people ask me if I remember the day it "all turned around for me?" "What caused me to change?" I tell them "Malnutrition!" It was really an understanding that service unlocks the front door of *the Bank of Providence*. The *Law of Cause and Effect* (making a commitment, and sticking to it) opens wide, the doors for opportunity. I try to deposit regularly now, every day, watching for the *committed* people that need some help. I have learned that when you give your personal service to a qualified recipient, your bank gets loaded with luck. I do not lend money; that usually delays disappointment for people. But I give food, a helping hand, compassion, understanding, service, precious time or "just" hugs. Learn to give to the deserving and give a good sermon to the undeserving! Remember, leaders carefully consider the reality of *Cause and Effect*. You can only give so much; it is possible to overdo it. Unless you are in the ministry or a missionary, the priority for the leader is to take care of business. Remember, a leader first acquires discipline, then respect, and finally, money. You cannot give it unless you have it. So we should inject service wisely throughout the wealth building process. John Davison Rockefeller gave us one example when he vowed he would spend half his life achieving wealth and the second half giving it away. He exemplifies my mentor Cavett Robert's motto, *"Those things we do for ourselves die with us. Those things we do for others will live on forever."* Today, the John D. Rockefeller foundation seems to always be sponsoring something, somewhere, everywhere.

3 x 5 CARD

I have an account in the Bank of Providence.
It is full and I can withdraw from it at will.
I use the account frequently,
depositing and withdrawing blessings.
(Ask for help and offer help today.)

Psychological Principle #16
LEADERS LEARN
THE JOY & PAIN OF DISCIPLINE

In 1880, Brigadier General Lew Wallace published the "Greatest Novel of the nineteenth century." It is titled *BEN-HUR*, and since 1880, it has never been out of print. Sears Roebuck & Co. alone sold more than a million copies of the book. The story is about a Jewish prince of the house of Hur, who was wrongly accused of attempting to assassinate a Roman Governor. The prince's name is Judah Ben-Hur. They sentenced him to slavery in the galley, where he would spend his life pulling an oar for the Roman navy. One day, the leader of the fleet came aboard Judah's ship and saw "number 60," as they called him. As he inspected the rowers, he noticed that unlike the other slaves, Judah Ben-Hur was physically strong, "a mass of muscle, which in some movements, swelled and knotted, like kinking cords." The Roman leader was impressed with his ability at the oar. He would pull the great oar with "grace and ease of action," and when he returned it he would "bend" it with the push. The officer asked about the slave with an interest to use him in the games of Rome as a Gladiator. Upon inquiring, he discovered that the slave had been the "best rower." The officer then asked, "Of what disposition is he?" Reply:

"He is obedient; further I know not. Once he made

a request of me...He wished me to change him alternately from the right to left... He had observed that the men they had confined to one side become misshapen. He also said that some day of storm or battle there might be sudden need to change him and he might then be unserviceable."

Judah Ben-Hur had decided to live and not only survive, but thrive in his circumstances. Leaders do this; they do not just survive, they always thrive. Zirconias settle for complacency, because like the slaves of the oars, they resign themselves to their fate. To sit day in and day out to the beat of a Roman drum, is what happens to so many in our society today: doing the same non-duplicable things repeatedly; never believing it can get better; and never applying the DISCIPLINES necessary to get out of the rut. As we read in Lew Wallace's story:

"So, as the result of long service, (at the oars) the poor wretches became imbruted — patient, spiritless, obedient — creatures of vast muscle and exhausted intellects, who lived upon recollections, generally few but dear, and at last lowered into the semiconscious alchemic state wherein misery turns to habit, and the soul takes on incredible endurance." Judah Ben-Hur was driven by a vision of freedom. Though sentenced for life, he determined he would someday be free again, so he applied personal discipline.

Discipline is a major factor for achieving a state of happiness and freedom. It is the ability to do something again and again, and never lose the focus of the desired result. The problem is that people who have no vision of the end cannot maintain the disciplines of the present. They revert to the non-disciplined actions of the COMFORT zone (or CAPTIVE zone), and stop believing. They are but galley slaves, with other people dictating what they will do each day, and what they are worth. The Zirconia will adhere to this COMFORT zone, but tell *you* to do the work. Zirconias will seek an easy way out, a quick-fix trip to success. It will never happen. You can fall into fortune. You will never fall into success.

In earlier pages we wrote about passion; how important it is to be passionate about something and to bring it to pass. If you want faster success, get passionate about being disciplined. In the WBI, if you are passionate about the fact that the key to growth is sharing the opportunity with new people, then become an expert in disciplined recruiting. If you are timid or shy, why not build on that weakness and it will become the strength you will be known for. First, you will be successful, (because you will sponsor well.) Second, you will be great from the stage, telling your story about overcoming the challenge.

A Zirconia leader will not strive to discipline themselves, but will teach the Principles of Discipline at meetings. When the meeting is over, however, these "cookie
eaters" never do the hard work alone. (A "cookie eater" is
someone who regularly attends business opportunity presentations without guests.)

Demosthenes was a great orator of ancient Greece. He
desired to be a speaker, but he had a speech impediment.
He was also known for being feeble and having a stam-
mering voice. His discipline to acquire the skills he needed
took him to climbing mountains to gain strength and
stamina. He would fill his mouth with small stones and
practice speaking on the beach, gesturing at his audience,
the sea. He entered caves, shaved his head and studied. He
knew he could not be seen bald in public, so he would study
until his hair had grown. Many people will say there are
those with natural speaking abilities, but I believe the greatest talents are the developed talents. It was said of
Demosthenes, "He was looked upon as a person of no great
natural genius, but one who owed all the power and ability he had in speaking to labor and industry." Today, some
2,375 years later, we revere him as the "greatest" because
of the fact he earned his reputation and was not born to it.
So how does the grocery checker become rich and live in
her dreams on a Hawaiian beach? *Discipline.* How does the
below-average insurance salesman go from broke to mega-
wealthy in five years, after eleven years of failure? *Disci-*
pline! How does a beer salesman become a multi-million-
aire? *Discipline!* It is learning what you must do and then

doing it repeatedly. If you get delayed by a Zirconia in your climb to independence, then catalog it and move on without looking back.

GET PASSIONATE! William James said "In almost any subject, your passion for the subject will save you. If you care enough for a result, you will attain it. If you wish to be good, you will be good, If you wish to be rich, you will be rich. If you wish to be learned, you will be learned. Only you must really wish these things, and wish them with exclusiveness, and not wish on a hundred other incompatible things, just as strongly."

Psychological Principle #17
LEADERS HAVE EVERYTHING NEEDED FOR SUCCESS.

The information in this book requires re-reading. Each time you read these principles they should provoke within you a desire to study and ponder more about you and about your background. More importantly, it should inspire you to act on what you have learned. It is also important to remember that you must begin today. Put into action as many of the principles as you can or you will lose what you have gained. Lord Francis Bacon wrote:

> *"Crafty men condemn studies, simple men admire them, and WISE men use them."*

Jim Rohn wrote:

> *"Everything you need for your better future and success has already been written...it is all available. But guess what? Only three percent of the people have a library card. Wow, they must be expensive! No, they're free."*
> *"Ignorance is not bliss. Ignorance is poverty. Ignorance is devastation. Ignorance is tragedy."*

Around 950 B.C. King Solomon said:

> *"...and there is no new thing under the sun."*

With all this information, we certainly should be able to determine where we can go and what heights we can obtain if we have a strong enough desire. We can even determine how long it will take and what we will have to pay to get there. The question is, "Will we take action?"

General George Washington wrote in a letter in June of 1783:

> "The citizens of America, placed in the most enviable condition, as the sole lords and proprietors of a vast tract of continent, comprehending all the various soils and climates of the world, and abounding with all the necessaries and conveniences of life are now...acknowledged to be possessed of absolute freedom and independency...Here they are not only surrounded with everything that can contribute to the completion of private and domestic enjoyment, but heaven has crowned (them with) all its other blessings...Researches of the human mind after social happiness have been carried to a great extent; the treasures of knowledge acquired by the labors of philosophers, sages, and legislators, through a long succession of years are laid open for us...At this auspicious period, the United States came into existence as a nation; *and if their citizens should not be completely free and happy, the fault will be entirely their own.*"

Well then, if we have the information and we have the opportunity through the concept of MLM to achieve unlimited financial success — if we have the knowledge, the vehicle and freedom to surpass all boundaries of financial bondage, then what will hold us back? Could it be our lack of belief in ourselves as leaders? Can we cross this last bridge to success and believe we are the leaders of the future?

Actually, the first key to measuring your leadership ability is whether or not you are already acting on what you have read. Only you know if there is a stack of 3x5 cards on your desk and one in your pocket. Only you know if you are committing yourself to the leadership principles presented here. Only you know if you have new books to read or are beginning a success journal. Only you know if you are going to become a speed-reader, or try your hand at writing. Only you know if you have enrolled in a speech class or night school.

Although we may have never met, I believe in you. Whatever your circumstances are, I know you can achieve your dreams. So in this section, I will share with you a few more points that will help you see into your future — to see your own capacity to win.

Jim McNeely teaches a seminar on what he calls the Socio-Economic scale of experience. He draws a diagonal line on a chalkboard and places titles of various professions on the line at different levels, signifying income. For example, at the top of the line he writes "doctor" or "lawyer," and at the bottom of the line, he writes "part-time gas station attendant"; this demonstrates the broad differences in income. He then asks the audience to shout, "stop" as he slowly moves his finger up the line. Perhaps half way up the line, the mechanic or schoolteacher will say stop. He then points out that people have a tendency to approach only those people whose professions fall equal to theirs or below. These people have a strong fear approaching anyone whose income or profession is above theirs on the line. Then Jim draws a second line on the board and explains that this is the line of "experience" that people have in Network Marketing. He points out that doctors, lawyers and professional people, fall far below the people who have gained experience and money through Network Marketing. The teacher and janitor now are high on the line, above those whose high-paid, high-stressed jobs are killing them. Jim goes on to point out that doctors, lawyers, accountants, and senior-level executives are looking for home-based wealth building opportunities and are quitting their jobs to get into Network Marketing while no one who has a successful life through Network Marketing is quitting to get into the high-stress jobs on the top of the income line. So it is important to realize how much power, knowledge and experience you already have. You need to move forward, armed with the confidence that you are the expert in this field, even if you are not the person with letters after their name.

Only you can be the one who decides your level of success, but you must decide now. You cannot let circumstances get in your way. You must accept that it is possible to win, no matter what your past has been. So many examples of achievement are all around you.

MCNEELY FORMULA

Socio-Economic Scale

Doctor
Lawyer
Engineer
Accountant

☞ YOU

Teacher
Plumber
Carpenter

Secretary
Janitor
Store Clerk

WBI Knowledge Scale

☞ YOU

Doctor
Lawyer
Engineer
Accountant

For the past two years, I have had the opportunity to teach a Sunday school class at the church I attend in Las Vegas. It is a youth class and some of these kids grew up on the mean streets of this fast-paced city. One in particular deserves mentioning to make a point I am talking about.

MonicA is eighteen years old. (She spells her name uniquely, because she knows she is unique.) She is tall, slender and very attractive; she has striking black eyes that flash with energy when she looks at you. She was a particularly noisy student two years ago when I first began teaching the class. She had a strange confidence in her demeanor, and yet her unruliness spoke of a lack of self-esteem. Rather than get angry at her disturbances in my class, I focused many of my most provoking questions toward her and was often amazed at her brilliant insight. How could a sixteen-year-old have such insight to life? And if the insight was so good, why was she so disruptive? Why was the knowledge being hidden by her poor classroom behavior? I began to inquire about her family. It turned out that she had two loving parents and several brothers and sisters — all active in their church and community. Then came the first real point of interest to me, MonicA was black and her parents were white. Further inquiry and eventually an in-depth interview with MonicA revealed an incredible story of struggle and desire for personal success in life.

At the age of three, MonicA was living in a small apartment off the Las Vegas Strip with her birth mother, older brother and infant sister. Her natural father had left the family and each child had a common mother but different fathers. MonicA (at the age of three) was being harassed by a neighbor (a white male). Although I have no details of the abuse, there was enough of a basis for MonicA's mother to take serious action on her daughter's behalf. She killed the man in front of her children. That was the last time the children would be in the custody of either of their birth parents. For the next several years, she was shuffled from one foster family to another. She became fiercely independent and extremely rowdy. She bit teachers, counselors and "white people." She was separated from her brother and sister. After being in over twenty homes, she was finally placed (for the first time) with a white family. She and her counselor decided that in order for her to get over her deep-seated hatred, she needed to face her problem directly. For three years she struggled with this new foster family, but through endurance fueled by love and patience, positive bonds were finally established. Her social life at school was particularly trying. Eventually she found herself learning to overcome the criticism received when explaining to her peers why she had white parents. That can be a major identity crisis for a teenager in the streets of Las Vegas in the nineties. She learned to recognize that her family loved her. Race and background were not the issue in their relationship, unconditional love was. It was not easy. Even in high school she would, at times, get into fights and be kicked out of school. But that is not unusual for children raised under the best of circumstances.

What is the main point in my sharing this story with you? It is this:

MonicA should not be a high school graduate with plans to get her degree in Theater, English and Business. She should not be active in her church or be respected by her peers. In today's world, she should have been just another casualty of the city, but she chose to win. She held on without regard to what others thought. She faced her fears with all odds against her, determined to seek the high life, and not the low life. *I am willing to bet she will succeed in life*. I am willing to bet she will be a leader and an achiever. She has had every excuse to fail, but she held on until she found help. The help she accepted was once her greatest fear, but became her greatest asset.

MonicA has changed her last name and has been adopted into her "real" family. It required getting permission from her natural mother and father, which they gave. She has chosen what *she* wants. She has determined what she can and will do. All these important decisions required her to make *choices* and stand by them.

Truly, we do have everything we need for success. If we have made up our minds to take our lives to the outer limits, it is up to us. Start by acting on what you know! Beware of the Zirconias that will have all the advice available, have read all the books, been to all the seminars, and accomplished nothing! They are out there in force waiting for you. They are full of free advice, cheap advice, and some will even let you finance the fee for their advice! What a deal!

Psychological Principle #18
LEADERS HAVE REAL GOALS
AND
THEY ACHIEVE THEM.

It is said that people can fall into fortune, but they cannot fall into success. I believe this to be true; success and happiness can only be earned. In looking back on my own life and the lives of the successful people I have studied over the years, there is one major difference between people who have goals, and those who do not. People who have goals and strive to achieve them, are much happier and fulfilled in their lives and they generally end up much wealthier. The same is true for all the Network Marketers I have met. The ones with balanced goals are simply happier than those without balance. The money was not an issue, except to say those with goals obtained their money faster and usually in greater abundance.

As I read about people who appeared to have succeeded in their careers, but were miserable, I sought to discover if indeed they had goals, or were they just talented people? How happy was Vincent Van Gogh? He was a marvelous artist, but history portrays him as a very unhappy man. How fulfilled was Edgar Allen Poe? How much joy lifted Beethoven? Was happiness a way of life for Herman Melville? Great artists, poets, composers, and writers, all incredibly talented, but happy? The question looms as we study their lives.

Julian Hawthorn said of Melville:

> "...(he) had pretty much made up his mind to be annihi-
> lated; but still he does not seem to rest in that anticipa-
> tion; and, I think, will never rest until he gets hold of a
> DEFINITE BELIEF."

These great people achieved unbelievable things in their lifetimes, but if they would have used the modern approach of goal setting, one wonders if even greater heights would have been achieved. Not only in the accomplishments they aspired to, but in their personal lives, in their social and family lives, and in their financial lives. Our ability today, to understand balance and organization is superior to that of any age in recorded history. Although we marvel at the achievements of entire civilizations from the Egyptian to the Mayan, I believe if you were to be catapulted back through time with a daily planner and a few books, you would be held up as a royal counsel to the Pharaoh.

Goal setting is a nuisance to a teenager. It is a lesson in life for the college student and a necessary evil for business managers. It is a lifesaver for the young executive, and a way of life for the C.E.O. of a company. But, *it is an art form in the hands of the Wealth Building millionaire!*

So where do you find the perfect system for setting goals? You won't find it here. This book contains no specific systems. It contains only principles you need to master. Many good books on how to organize your life and establish goals are available. Leaders search out what will work for them and they know the system that is best for them, because it will be the one they use! We must accept however, that the primary need in being able to move forward is a strong determination to change and to become focused and organized. Otherwise, the trite philosophies we laugh about are the anchors that keep us from our dreams.

"If things don't change, they'll stay the same!"

It was Alexander Pope circa 1735, who said, *"Blessed is he who expects nothing, for he shall never be disappointed!"*

Perhaps the best phrase I have enjoyed yet, is one that addresses those lonely Zirconias that have no goal, but love to complain about how miserable life is anyway. Described vividly by George Elliot circa 1860:

"An ass may bray ("Heehaw!") a good while before he shakes the stars down!"

I have found a few profound lessons that when followed can bring about remarkably fast results.

Lesson #1: Decide WHAT You Want.

First, you must decide on something you want, but do not have. The definition of the word "problem," that I have adopted, is the "difference between what people have and what they want!" It has been pointed out that in our modern society, there are more televisions than there are bathtubs. We are a "want" generation, and we will do amazing things to get what we want. Most people today think they work for the ABC company, but in reality, most folks work for only four conglomerates: Visa®, MasterCard®, American Express®, and Mr. Mortgage! So as you begin to determine what it is that you want, take into consideration more than just the "want" and "have" aspects of your dream, take into account the "feel" and "freedom" part also.

As you are determining your main goal (or want), remember that there are good goals and bad ones. Bad ones always lead to some kind of bondage. Good ones always lead to freedom. So your first good goal may be to have a bank account with $50,000 cash, *unencumbered,* in it. This is a worthy and worthwhile goal. The figure could be $5,000 cash or it could be a $250,000. The amount is only relevant to you. But it must be measurable, achievable, and what you really want.

✎ Important Note *◣*

You must believe you can achieve it. You must also have reference points of those who have done it before you. If you do not, it is probably not a realistic goal, and you should re-establish it.

Lesson #2: Decide WHEN You Want It!

Everyone has one major role in life and many intermediate goals in between. To obtain any goal, we must establish timetables. So let's begin with the major goal and divide it by the months, weeks, and days it will take to achieve it. It is imperative that you have a timetable. To simplify this example, consider that you can afford to save $500 per month; it would take you 100 months to save your goal amount of $50,000.

That would be approximately 8.3 years, 432 weeks, or 3021 days. Your responsibility now has a broader scope to examine. From a different angle, it is about $16.50 per day or $115 per week.

Well, the goal which sounded so exciting is looking more and more unrealistic, right? It can get worse if you are not prepared to really get into the FEAR zone.

You see, you are probably not out of debt, right?

Let us say you are in debt to the tune of $100,000 including your home. You will need another 16 years calculated in straight math, to pay off bills before you can amass the goal. This is the information that can send the Zirconia right back to the television with a can of cheap beer and a resolve that those "home-based business deals" never work.

They just get you pumped up and then they fizzle out!

The supporting precept here is: *are you willing to pay the price of success?* It is a stretch. It is a reach. Can you reach your goal? If you can believe it, you can have it!

Now that you have done the realistic work that 90 out of 100 MLM distributors are unwilling to do, you are ready to face the reality and possibility of reaching the dreams you are wanting. If you have overcome the temptation to throw your hands up and say, "Forget it. It is too hard!" Then you are ready for the next lesson.

As you begin breaking down the time and counting the cost, your main goal will expand into many objectives that must be reached first. You will need a method to get the extra $500 per month. So you will need to leverage your time after work into your Network Marketing business. You will have to help others get what *they* want in order to achieve success in *your* business. You will have to become a good teacher; learn how to do home meetings; and become an expert in the techniques of multi-level marketing. You will be working in the system you choose, a system that works for you. You must always keep your eye on the main goal, ever moving forward with your primary objectives taking you step by step closer to your main goal of $50,000 in the bank (or whatever your goal is.) As you can see, the main goal provides the beacon that you will keep your eyes on as you organize all the necessary forces to win the prize. It is your WHY, your reason to go to work each day. By seeking a goal that requires others to succeed in order for you to succeed, your goal is truly a WORTHY GOAL, regardless of the product or service you offer. People with such goals are not imprisoned by time clocks or shackled by calendars; they are driven by dedication and enthusiasm. They understand that killing time is not a minor crime; it is suicide. They have resolved that if there is any killing of time to be done in their lives, it will be by working it to death. Remembering the timely words of the industrialist Kettering:

"I don't want a man who has a ~~job~~.(GOAL) I want a man whom a ~~job~~ (GOAL) has — has so completely in its grasp

that it is the last thing he thinks about at night before he closes his eyes. It has him so completely under its spell that each morning when he wakes up it is sitting on the side of the bed beckoning him to arise and partake of the joys and adventures of his work."

Lesson #3: Goal-Oriented Leaders Work Hard and Accept Help.

The next thing you must have is a desire to recruit the universe to your cause! Leverage your time, talents and focus, to make the dream come true. Believe that when you become committed, the world around you will begin to recognize your resolve and join you in your crusade. This third lesson encompasses several supporting precepts. If understood, these precepts can speed up the entire process, often cutting the time of accomplishment to one tenth, in exchange for ten times the effort! One supporting precept is best explained by Benjamin Disraeli:

"The best way to become acquainted with a subject is to write a book about it."

We're not going to recommend that you write any books, but we do suggest you *become an expert* in the goal you are pursuing.

I was told of a story of a minister that was walking his neighborhood in search of inactive members of his congregation. Knocking on a door he met an elderly woman who had given up on life. She was a shut-in, miserable and bitter; her house was unkempt. She was alone and feeling sorry for herself. The minister, not knowing what to say to her (with her advanced age and no relatives to help), suggested she wake up the next day and study about the first thing she saw. The following morning, as she was opening the back door to get the milk off her porch, she noticed the brick steps. She remembered the advice of the minister. She looked up the word "brick" in the dictionary. Then she looked in her encyclopedia for "brick." She dressed for the first time in months and walked to her local library. Along the way, she noticed for the first time, the myriad of different styles of bricks used in her neighborhood. She discovered that bricks were first made eons ago. The idea came from "mud cakes" left in river bottoms of dry rivers. Ancient man would stack the cakes up to build crude houses. Later, the first recorded brick-making began around 6000 B.C. By 4000 B.C. organized brick-making had begun. She learned about the Egyptians, the Romans and the difference between their styles. She studied about how bricks were made from clay, river mud, sand and asphalt, lime, concrete and glass. She learned about colors and textures. She smashed long-held beliefs. She had always pictured the Great Wall of China made totally of stone, but much of it was sun dried and burnt brick. On and on went her studies. They rejuvenated her spirits and she rose each morning eager to get to the library. She learned how enameling began in 600 B.C.

She would close her eyes and travel inside her mind to the Nile, Tigris, and Euphrates rivers imagining their evolution from mud huts to today's concrete houses. Can a simple goal to become an expert change a life? Yes! And it will change yours.

This great lady did not compare her task to someone else's accomplishment. It was her goal and her task. Its magnitude and greatness was manifested in her, and she determined its greatness and value. Helen Keller stated:

"I long to accomplish a great and noble task. But is my chief duty to accomplish humble tasks as though they were great and noble. The world is moved along, not only by the mighty shoves of its heroes, but also by the aggregate of the tiny pushes of each honest worker."

Whatever you choose as a goal, drive with passion and eagerness to achieve. It will, in the end, be a great accomplishment in the eyes of the world. So start!

Can you become an expert on what compound interest can do to $16.50 per day? Can you figure a way to make the $50,000 in one year? Can you become an expert on "DUPLICATION," as did one retired Canadian policeman (R.C.M.P.) who achieved an income of over a quarter-million-dollars-a-year in less than three years? Can you become an expert on time-management? On goal achievement? On the magic of affirmations? How about on a particular product or healing method? Or the history of the *Wealth Building Industry?* There are a million subjects that will directly relate to your goal. Whatever your goal is, become an expert on the subject.

Another supporting precept of utmost importance is working fast and hard. Remember Thomas Edison's wonderful quote:

"Everything comes to him who hustles while he waits."

Another way I have heard this put is, "All things come to those who only stand and wait, but it's leftovers from those who hustled!" In Voltaire's writings we have the famous riddle:

> *"What is the longest and yet the shortest?*
> *The Swiftest and yet the slowest.*
> *All of us neglect it. Then we all regret it.*
> *Nothing can be done without it.*
> *It swallows up all that is small,*
> *And it builds up all that is great?"*

The answer to the riddle of course, is *Time*. Long in eternity, yet none of us have enough of it. Swift in enjoyment and forever, when in pain. We all neglect it. And of course, we cannot live without more of it tomorrow. It swallows and forgets us if we remain small, but builds us in the eternities if we *do something to be remembered!*

The *Wealth Building Industry* offers the average person the chance to be great; to really do something; and to genuinely uplift peoples' lives. It motivates people to become greater than they are. Our short lives need this business over all other methods of business offered to the masses. We each have a very limited window of time to really do something. Something BIG! BIG, to me, means something that will help others — thousands of others. Because the time factor is too short, we have to hustle, get going and start today! Let us not be like Methuselah (in the Bible) who lived for 969 years, and to my best recollection, leaves us nothing as a legacy for his time spent here.

In our lifetime, we only have a few productive years to do something; to set a good goal and see it through; to teach someone how to be successful and to get the most out of the precious moments we have on this spinning orb. Let us begin today!

So, decide *what* you truly want! Then decide *when* you want it. Then commit to *work hard* and stay focused. *Accept the help* that will come to you, as it will. Break the time down and make sure you are willing to pay the price. Don't be afraid to dream big. And don't be afraid to do the menial tasks at hand. I know people who have accomplished being out of debt and having $50,000 in the bank without it taking years. One man did it in nine months. A friend of mine, in Florida, did it in four years. You can accomplish your goal much quicker than you plan to if you accelerate your efforts and apply supreme enthusiasm. So work hard and accept help. If you want to accelerate the success process, work harder and faster. Do all you can and then, a little bit more!

Psychological Principle #19
LEADERS ONLY "LOOK BACK" FOR WISDOM.

As you read the concluding principles of this book, realize you are not a Zirconia. You are a Diamond. You are the most precious gem on the planet. You are denied nothing. Every good thing on earth is available to you. It is all waiting. Every physical thing, emotional feeling, and spiritual experience is waiting for you to step up and purchase it. You can pay with your time, your money, your work, or your service. Nothing will be denied you.

In 1952 an unhappy couple was driving through the Nevada desert, when they stopped at a bar to have a drink. As they went in, they told their oldest son to keep an eye on the other three children in the back seat. As one drink led to another, the night warmed up in the bar, but it got colder and colder for the children in the car. During the night, the temperature fell to freezing, and the fourteen-year-old boy covered his two-year-old youngest brother with soiled rags and newspapers for warmth. The three older children huddled together and shivered in the night air. As the dawn broke, and the sun began to peer over the horizon, the parents came back out and without concern, drove on.

When I first heard this story I marveled at how such people could get away with such poor parental behavior. But the story goes on. The young man held grudges as he grew and the parents became more and more miserable in their downward spiraling life of alcoholism. Four years later, the mother shot herself. The father did his best to raise the four children, but fighting his own demons made parenting an exercise in survival, and nothing more. I was the infant that had been wrapped in the oily rags that cold night in Nevada. Eventually it was my older brother, Ira who took my father into his home, as was mentioned earlier in the book.

Many years later, I asked my brother how he got over that memory. I asked how it was that he could excuse our parent's actions and move on. He told me on a long drive through the Washington countryside, that if we use things that happen to us as an excuse not to perform, we are victims of circumstance instead of creators of it. We are then controlled by an unseen force that keeps us from reaching our full human potential. That night, we were on our way to an appointment for a network marketing presentation. We drove two hours, and then two hours back home again. The people never signed up.

As time moved on, my mother was gone, and my father worked as a long-haul truck driver for most of the rest of his life. Eventually, my entire family moved away. And I would rarely see or hear from them.

How easy it would have been to use these experiences as excuses. But I was told, "Leaders don't make excuses." I heard Dean Naylor once state, "You can make excuses, or you can make money, but you can't make both!" Dean is retired from the *Wealth Building Industry* and lives in a beautiful home on a lake in Idaho. He has time and money freedom and lives the lifestyle that most people only dream about. His personal story of overcoming difficulty in life is as tough as they come, but Dean flourished through his adversities. He used his past only for the wisdom gained, not as a crutch to hobble on. I would not know any events of his past, except he told the story once in the six years that I have known him. Many people can't get through the day without complaining about some event that happened to them twenty years prior.

Psychological Principle #20
LEADERS REFLECT ON LIFE AND ITS LESSONS.

I have spent very few precious moments with my family growing up, but I have used these memories over the years to learn from and help others. *I believe the primary experience you need to build a Network Marketing business is the experience you have already gained in life.* I can draw confidence to battle the daily challenges in building a successful organization by remembering events of my past. I ask myself, *"What did I learn here?" "How did it shape me into who I am today?"* I challenge you to do this. As you begin to rediscover your lessons from your past, take notes. By sharing personal stories in your trainings, you endear people and teach them to search their past for the wisdom forgotten. Success principles in life are the same for business and you simply must apply them to reap the rewards. For example, I went to a scout jamboree when I was 12 years old. My father told me to win any race I might be in. He never attended any activities I participated in at church, scouts or school. He did, however, expect me to win and I did not want to disappoint him (creative expectancy). I was a radical Boy Scout who thought the leaders wished I would not show up. I wore an old pair of cowboy boots and did not own a uniform. Our troop was smaller than the others were; we did not believe we could win the "litter race." The race required us to cut three poles and tie them together to build an "Indian litter" (to be pulled behind a pony). Then, with one boy on the litter, the other two would drag the litter fifty yards over a line and then back to win. I championed the race, because I *had* to tell my dad we won. When the race started, we cut and tied the litter and dragged it up and down the race course so fast, none of the other troops had made it off the starting line. We lost! We were disqualified! We found out the reason we were so fast was we did not use any scout knots. We did not even know any scout knots! I protested loudly and demanded a re-run. After all, no one had explained any "knot rules" to me! I asked if there was one knot that would work for each joint and they said, "Yes." I then asked if someone could teach it to us. We practiced for five minutes and then re-ran the race. We won the race before anyone had left the starting line. *I learned the leadership principle of DETERMINATION at age 12. I also learned not give up or QUIT. I learned that when you are committed, FOLLOW THROUGH!*

On another occasion, my father and I were heading out on one of our rare fishing trips in the Arizona mountains. He would drive our old '58 pickup to the edge of town and then ask me if I wanted to drive. I was under age, but that did not stop him or me. In a second, I was behind the wheel and he was next to me helping me get the truck going in first gear. Then I took over.

He would take a "nip" on a bottle of clear liquid and soon be snoring away. On one occasion, I woke him and asked him how he drove so near the edge of the road without going over the edge? He was mildly disturbed that I had bothered him, but he said, "Just put your right wheel on the white line and drive down the right side of the road." The answer was too simple. I had not made myself clear. I then asked if he used the right fender as a guide to determine where the edge of the road was. He said "No. Just drive down the white line on the right side of the road." I pondered a bit further, and then asked if the angle of the hood ornament when aligned with the edge of the road was held at an angle of... He interrupted me with an explosive shout, "JUST DRIVE DOWN THE WHITE LINE ON THE RIGHT SIDE OF THE ROAD!" Before he finished speaking, I had the wheel on the white line and drove quietly all the way to the fishing hole with no further interruptions. Leaders just DO IT! They rarely ask why or whine, they just drive down the white line.

I asked my dad if he ever read a book. He said he had read 264 books! I said "Wow!" and asked him when he read them. I had never seen him read anything but the Bible, on Sundays. He said that was what he had read: the Bible, four times. (66 books of old and new testament x 4 = 264) A leader reads and becomes an expert on something.

I asked my father why my older sister was such a "pain." She was the only girl of the four children and no mother in the home. My father said, "Son there are deer in the forest, dogs in the streets and birds in the trees. There are little boys and little girls. They are all different, and that's why they act differently. As for your sister, it is just the nature of the beast, son, that's all, just the nature of the beast."

At the time I never understood what he meant, but after 22 years of marriage and 5 children, *I learned that it is not my job to change people around me, but instead, I need to change me around people. People are people and leaders accept everyone without judgement as potential leaders. Leaders judge actions, not people.*

As for distributors that we often refer to as "disturb-a-tors," or "distribu-terrorists," well, it is just the nature of the beast. *A leader would never let another person's actions deter them from building their dream.*

On another camping trip, I remember two incidents that taught me distinctive lessons on "No Fear" and "No Barriers." The trip started out typically. I started driving outside of town and dad started snoring. After an hour of driving, we were passing through a small town and I woke dad and told him we had forgotten to pack any food. We could eat fish tomorrow, but what about tonight? He had me pull into a grocery store. He had enough gas to get us home and two extra dollars. He bought a whole chicken, a roll of tin foil, and some salt and pepper (those tiny ones you rarely see anymore). He seasoned the chicken, wrapped it in tin foil and stuck it under the carburetor, on the intake manifold of our Studebaker. When we arrived at the fishing hole, the chicken was cooked and ready to eat. On another occasion, we could not afford the foil so he just threw the chicken into the fire. After a short time, he dug it out with a stick. Under a quarter inch of black charcoal, was a delightful tender roasted chicken. A leader finds a way. A leader asks for help. A leader understands humble does not mean unhappy.

My father taught me to pray at a young age, he said God will always help me if I needed him. I asked him if he ever had a prayer answered, and he said, "Many." I inquired further for an example, and he said he lost his top (toy with a string) when he was my age. He prayed about it. He said God knew where it was, and he wanted it...now! He said a "force" pushed his hand under the bed, and "way into the corner." There he found his top. He thanked God and went out to play.

Leaders listen intently to even the newest of distributors. They give only information that can help them on the level they are on. Leaders empathize.

After the death of my mother — because there were no witnesses, and my mother used a gun to take her life — my father was investigated for her death. My mother's family all believed my dad was responsible, because the authorities were involved, even though that was a standard investigative procedure. My dad was miserable. He had four children to raise, and no companion. He told me in later years that in his agony, he went to a park and prayed as he walked. "What should I do? What can I do?" he asked. As he was walking, a bent over bum held out his hand and asked my father for a dime. My father blew up, and in a rage he yelled, "My life is falling apart, my wife is gone, my children are afraid, and you want a dime? Why don't you just get a job and be responsible!" He told me an amazing transformation took place before his eyes. The man stood up, and was taller than my father was. He straightened out his overcoat, and kind of dusted himself off. He said to my father "Okay, I understand." Then he turned and walked away. His walk was powerful and not the shuffling gait of the typical homeless person. Suddenly my father realized he had received the answer to his prayer. He had rejected it as soon as he heard it. He told me he ran to the man, grabbed his coat, and dropping to his knees, asked the man to please take all the money that he had. It was not much, mostly coins. He held them out with both hands, on his knees, before this "bum" as he worded it. The man said, "Thank you" to him and took only a dime. My dad pleaded for him to take it all, but the man would only take a dime.

My father held this story sacred for most of his life, only revealing it to me, as far as I am aware of. Perhaps he told other members of my family, I don't know. But he always felt that when he prayed, he got answers. And when he asked "What should I do" to curb the pain and misery of his life, the answer was to *SERVE OTHERS.* The answer came almost instantaneously with an opportunity to help someone else without judgement at that very moment. He said "I almost missed the answer." It reminded me of the many times he would see deer in the woods and point them out to me. I always wondered why he saw them first, but it was because he was looking for them and I was not. *Leaders look for opportunities to serve. Leaders do not care who gets the credit. Leaders are often alone in their quest.*

My life is full now –full of joy and wonder. I am surrounded with excitement and adventure. I am blessed with five wonderful children from a happy marriage approaching a quarter-of-a-century in length. Our time together is always too short as we travel and enjoy life. I teach two Sunday school classes in my church, pondering the mysteries of eternal possibilities. As a speaker, I address the greatest people on earth. I challenge them to be more, do more, and contribute more. I snowboard with my children and scuba dive in exotic places with my friends from all over the continent. I sail away in my art. I write my books and poems knowing I need only to please myself. I am even trying to learn a song for a karaoke performance I might do some day. (Now that is a scary challenge for me!) I listen to music and practice the piano, the trumpet and the harmonica. (I believe my kids think I am quite accomplished, because they keep encouraging me with, "Keep practicing dad! Keep practicing!") I still have the entanglements of life as we all do, but they are just more opportunities to grow and develop. I awake everyday with a purpose to rise and jump into the day. I am still learning to be a better husband — to quit questioning why flowers are important and just buy them. I have even taken up ballroom dancing (my wife likes to dance.) I am working on being a better dad and trying to understand why my kids are not perfect! What is wrong with *them* anyway? I strive daily to support our distributorship which currently spans 50 states and three countries. I have learned that advanced leadership makes a distributor a crusader with a worthy quest. A quest to release people shackled by misery and complacency. I traveled 300,000 miles last year and covered 25,000 in the first six weeks of this year. I do some consulting and produce motivational tapes for the *Wealth Building Industry* (WBI). I never miss a school conference or play that my children are involved in. In all of this, I am fulfilled and happy, because I have learned to apply the principles of leadership. As they say in our business, "If *he* can do it, *anyone* can do it!" In spite of his weaknesses, I had a great dad (I believe he looks in on me from time to time). I have an incredible wife who has lived the trying life of being married to an entrepreneur who is full of "wonder and wander." I am driven by a powerful WHY that pushes me on in a dedicated mission to encourage you to be the best you can be.

So where does the training come from for you to win? You already have it. It is the sugar in your teacup waiting for you to stir things up and get things going. It is all inside you or available from books, tapes, and life. Success is yours, if you will just claim it. Take ownership and be a little patient for its possession, and it will come. You will sleep good at night and dream the special dreams reserved for those rare few who dare to make a difference in such a troubled world. You will sleep peacefully knowing that you have spent your days attempting to enrich the lives of others. You have the greatest opportunity to help others find financial and time freedom. Have pride in your business and be proud of your cause. Become a teacher and yet, remain a student. As prosperity and happiness come your way, share them with others as often as you can. Remember:

"Those things we do for ourselves die with us.
Those things we do for others will live on forever."

NOTES

NOTES